# Hero

by

Brandon Scott Elrod
&
Desiree Elrod

Ravenhill Publishing

ISBN-10: 0983149577
ISBN-13: 978-0-9831495-7-6

First Printing: 2018

Ravenhill Publishing
Santa Ana, California

To our children;

May you always remember

that you were made in the image of God

and He has an incredible destiny

awaiting you.

**Chapter 1—The Opening Scene** .................................................................. **11**
You are part of an epic story............................................................. 12
What are we missing? ....................................................................... 13
The Adolescent Heart of a Future Hero............................................. 15
Sin and Wounding in the Hero........................................................... 16

**Chapter 2—Prayer: Messages from the King** .......................................... **19**
What is your prayer life like? ............................................................ 21
What exactly is prayer?..................................................................... 23
Aligning with the Father.................................................................... 24
Hearing God...................................................................................... 25
What does it mean to "hear God?"..................................................... 27

**Chapter 3—Your Backstory: the growth of False Self**...................…………..………**31**
Your Backstory.................................................................................. 33
Your False Self.................................................................................. 34
False Self as our Filter....................................................................... 35
When Facades become Barriers......................................................... 38
Exchanging Barriers.......................................................................... 39

**Chapter 4—Yielding: The Hero is Emancipated**……………………………….**43**
It's time to give up............................................................................ 45
The agenda of False Self.................................................................... 46
Yielding ............................................................................................. 49
So Simple, but So Hard...................................................................... 51

**Chapter 5—True Identity: Sons and Daughters of the King** ..................... **53**
The significance of being a child of the King .................................... 56
A child of God: no big deal ............................................................... 57
Our Father's Discipline ..................................................................... 58
Intimacy with God ............................................................................ 61
Conclusion ........................................................................................ 63

**Chapter 6—True Identity: Soldiers of God**.............................................. **65**
Soldiers by design............................................................................. 68
Warrior vs. Soldier............................................................................ 68
Militia vs. Army ............................................................................... 69
Our Allies.......................................................................................... 70
Roll Call............................................................................................ 72

**Chapter 7—True Identity: Priests of God Most High**.............................. **75**

Children of the King are also priests. .................................................. 78

You and I are priests. ............................................................................ 78

Your Self: His Temple ......................................................................... 79

Your Spirit.............................................................................................. 80

Your Soul .............................................................................................. 85

Your Body.............................................................................................. 86

**Chapter 8—True Identity: Princes and Princesses ...................... 91**

A Royal Birthright ................................................................................ 94

Ambassadors for our Father.................................................................. 96

Walking circumspectly.......................................................................... 96

Being groomed to reign......................................................................... 97

**Chapter 9—True Identity: Spiritual Roles................................... 99**

You have a one-of-a-kind purpose. .................................................... 102

There is life beyond salvation............................................................. 103

The Five Spiritual Roles...................................................................... 104

The Model of Spiritual Roles............................................................... 106

Being Christ-like.................................................................................. 107

**Chapter 10—True Identity: Spiritual Gifts................................. 109**

You have been outfitted for the King's missions ............................... 113

Designed to be heroes ......................................................................... 114

How does it work?............................................................................... 116

Proper perspective on gifts ................................................................. 117

**Chapter 11—Identity Theft: Your True Name ........................... 119**

Who are you really?............................................................................. 123

God redefines and restores ................................................................. 125

Biblical characters and their True Identity.......................................... 125

The importance of struggle.................................................................. 126

Our Father is our Author ..................................................................... 127

**Chapter 12—Spiritual Authority................................................. 129**

You have been given authority to act on the King's behalf! ............... 131

The Opposite of Authority................................................................... 132

The Model of Authority ...................................................................... 133

Growing in Authority.......................................................................... 135

Conclusion .......................................................................................... 138

**Chapter 13—Calling ................................................................... 139**

What is your great kingdom assignment?......................................................... 140
What is Calling? ........................................................................................... 140
How are we called?....................................................................................... 141
Why are we called?....................................................................................... 143
What is expected of those who are called? ..................................................... 143
Why are we afraid of Calling?....................................................................... 144

# Chapter One

## The Opening Scene

There once was a young boy who lived in a forest cottage. He was a curious lad, and he always found it more fascinating to escape into the trees than to pick up after himself, or bathe in the pond. Jonathan's life in the forest was not all that different from the other children nearby.

His dearest friend was a girl in the woods. She was not at all like him, rather, she was determined and driven. When they would play among the ferns of the forest, scampering over logs and boulders, it would be his curiosity and her persistence that spurred them on to accomplish anything the other could do. Jonet[*] and Jonathan[†] were inseparable.

Life in Freeman's Forest—as the children called it—must have seemed idyllic. Aside from the normal obligations of life, like putting yourself to bed, or collecting food, there wasn't much to be concerned with or alarmed by. The children just existed, and never really wondered how they got there or why they were alone. Loneliness was a way of life: like a vapor, of sorts, that was always present but was never truly identifiable. No one really *belonged* here.

Between the edge of the forest and the fortified wall of the city stretched the Fields of Plenty. Hardly a great description was the word *plenty*, though. For you see, although the field outside the great wall was constantly replenished with baskets of food, jugs of juice, and yes, even desserts and candies, it never seemed very fresh. Nowadays, we might call the bread *day-olds*, as it was a bit on the hard side; and the vegetables were just a little too soft, with the wrinkles that are often found on wilting produce. But there was a lot of it, so the children would never go hungry.

---

* Jonet meaning: God is gracious
† Jonathan meaning: God has given

11

Jonathan and Jonet took their daily jaunt into the field. They traipsed along between stacks of bread and around baskets of squishy vegetables, before stopping at the carrots, which looked firmer than the ones they had bypassed on their previous visit. And despite the unending supply of food, the young boy and girl—like all the other children in the forest—began to feel a hunger that could not be satisfied deep within their gut.

Such was the daily life of Jonathan and Jonet. It was a picture of independence, yes, but of loneliness. It was full of play and indulgence, but devoid of passion or purpose. And slowly—steadily—a sense of discontent started pulsing through their veins.

## Reading between the lines

In our simple allegory, Jonathan and Jonet represent two people who have never encountered God nor surrendered themselves to Him. They have not experienced transformation, and they do not bear fruit. Perhaps they are unsaved; perhaps they are *cultural Christians*. Although they are wired differently from each other, both are stuck in the same old uneventful life. There are plenty of distractions and diversions to keep them occupied, and both of them consume in a constant supply—though neither one ever feels truly satisfied.

But where are the adults in our allegory? And why are they missing? And what is the great wall protecting the children from? And why—despite having all of their physical needs met—why do they feel increasingly unfulfilled, like something significant is missing from their existence?

## You are part of an epic story.

There is an epic story unfolding here: *your story*. Having said this, I know what you're probably thinking. "There is nothing epic about my life."

So many Christians live life subconsciously looking for greatness. The trouble is that we look for it in *other* people. We foist our hopes and dreams on church leaders, figureheads, and political hopefuls. We read biographies of "heroes of the faith" and we long to be like them. Perhaps we even resign ourselves that it is impossible for us to be like them; that God must have had something special in mind when He made *them*. We, however, are the directionless masses. Our job is to follow orders and maybe, just maybe, we will find some fulfillment as we live vicariously through *that* missionary, *that* theologian, *that* pastor, *that* revolutionary— *that* man or *that* woman.

Are you spiritually hungry and thirsty? Does there seem to exist a great void in your Christianity? Perhaps it is missing the life it is supposed to have! In an ironic sense, that is great news, and acknowledging our need is a significant place to be! Jesus says, *"Blessed are those who hunger and thirst for righteousness..."*[*] He goes on to say, *"Whoever drinks of the water I give him shall never thirst; but the water that I will give him will become a well of water springing up to eternal life."*[†] He then explains what this eternal life is: *"This is eternal life, that they may know You, the only true God, and Jesus Christ, whom You have sent."*[‡]

Eternal life is knowing the Father, and it is knowing the Son, Jesus Christ. This, explains Jesus, is what will satisfy our thirst. If your experience is anything like the Christians we have talked with over the years, you probably feel relatively well acquainted with Jesus. Right? In church, we study Jesus, we examine His teachings, we launch campaigns to behave like Jesus behaved, and we center ourselves completely upon Him as our point of reference. This is good. But, it is only *part* of the story. *"This is eternal life, that they may know You..."*

Do you know the Father? If you are spiritually thirsty, dry, and lifeless, it may be that you have never gotten to know Him.

## What are we missing?

Jesus said, *"He who believes in Me, the works that I do, he will do also; and greater works than these he will do...If you ask anything in My name (on My behalf, in My authority), I will do it...I will ask the Father, and He will give you another Helper, that He may be with you forever."*[§]

Why don't we experience this? Some would say Jesus was only talking to His disciples; but why would He promise them the Holy Spirit indefinitely when none of them would live past the end of the first century? Some would say that "greater works" refers to quantity, not quality: *more* people have been saved, *more* taught, *more* ministered to after Jesus's life than

---

[*] Matthew 5:6
[†] John 4:14
[‡] John 17:3
[§] John 14:12-16

13

during. What I hear in all of this is an empty attempt to justify why we don't experience this first-hand. The truth is, God is actively and consistently engaged in supernatural work, all around us, and He loves to include us in it. We'll dive deeper into this later on in the book also.

So, the first question we should ask is, "Why don't our efforts work?" Actually, the better question is, "Why don't our efforts produce supernatural results?" The Adolescent is the Christian who is all about his own effort, his own intelligence, his own self-control, and his own motives. When the Adolescent "labors for God," is he really doing what God would have him do? Are his efforts producing fruit, or are they truly only *his* energy, *his* empowerment, and *his* agenda? Is he simply another Don Quixote, dressed in armor and suited up for battle, but charging inexplicably at windmills?

Inevitably, there are some recognizable characteristics of an Adolescent in the faith:

1. He is fearful of his calling. Don't we assume the worst about our Father, as if He knows the most dreaded task and setting we could imagine, and has made that our calling?
2. She has no victory over sin. Despite our efforts, we keep repeating the same things in an endless sin-repent-repeat cycle.
3. He does not know how to be a spiritual leader. This is a major area of fear for the Christians we have talked with. What does it mean? How do you do it? How do you know if you are doing it well?
4. She does not recognize God's activity—she rationalizes. We complain that God seems distant, yet when He involves Himself in the moments of our lives, do we give Him the credit for it?
5. He does not know the voice of God, and therefore, does not experience intimacy with Him. When God speaks,[*] we don't recognize it as Him; when we await His response, we overlook His reply. We then assert that "God doesn't speak anymore except through Scripture," as a way to validate our lack of hearing.
6. She knows all about God, yet she does not know Him. Just like the Pharisees,[†] we can recite passage after passage about God, yet we completely miss Him in spite of our knowledge.

---

[*] John 10, Hebrews 3:7-8
[†] John 5:39-40

This Adolescent living is a state we all must pass through; it is formative to our spiritual development. But, the ultimate destination is beyond it— deep in the territory of Fatherhood and Motherhood, where oneness and abiding bring intimacy with the Father. It is where the Father invites each one of us. And inevitably, we all must come to the fork in the road at the end of Adolescence.

## The Adolescent Heart of a Future Hero

For the sake of our developing story, the hero—you—must begin a new chapter: one of introspection. You see, it is unavoidable; God always invites His people into this process if He is going to release them into their destiny. Why is this? Your destiny is dependent on your identity, and in order to discover your identity, you must throw open the curtains that have darkened the dusty corners of *you*. You must allow the light to stream in and reveal what it will. How does this sit with you? Does it create anxiety? Fear? Anger? Excitement? Relief?

It is important, at this point, to identify which *you* we are talking about. The Scriptures refer to this *you* in two main terms throughout the Old Testament and the New: soul and heart. Both of these words are used interchangeably. The Greek word for heart here is *psyche*, which is clearly a term that has found modern use. So, soul, heart and psyche are, hereafter, referring to the same thing. For ease of conversation, I will use the word soul as we move forward.

The soul is the seat of your intellect, your emotion/experience, and your will. It is a theme that the authors of Scripture acknowledged repeatedly, and every once in a while, you will see them appear together in context. Here are two examples:

*"But just as you abound in everything, in faith and utterance and knowledge (intellect), and in all earnestness and in the love we inspired in you (emotions), see that you abound in this gracious work also (will)." 2 Corinthians 8:7*

These verses begin to lay a foundation for us: the solid base that comes when our soul is *in alignment*. In other words, when there is agreement between our intellect, emotions and will. This implies, of course, that the opposite is true: we can exist in a state of internal disagreement. Is this you? Do you sense that inside your soul there exists an unresolved conflict?

This is important to recognize! When our intellect, emotions and will are disjointed from each other, the result is that we cannot live in authenticity, in wholeness. Our only option is to live incompletely, misaligned internally, which means that part of us is being misrepresented, minimized, or lied about. This state of non-authenticity is referred to as our False Self.

Our False Self is the result of internal conflict and lack of health. It happens to all of us. Any wound our soul has ever experienced has driven a wedge between our intellect, emotions and will. And, the longer we live in this state, and the stronger the wound, the harder it is for us to rediscover our True Identity. In other words, the harder it is to let go of the old man and put on the new man.

## Sin and Wounding in the Hero

Many Christians have no problem being forthcoming about their sin; it is the wounding that makes people clam up. Some of us admit we have wounds, but minimize their importance, while others refuse to acknowledge wounds at all.

The trouble with minimizing, or denying for that matter, is that we exclude ourselves from Jesus's mission. In Luke 4, Jesus announced the mission He had come to fulfill, and it was robust. Quoting from Isaiah 61:

*"The Spirit of the Sovereign LORD is on me, because the LORD has anointed me to preach good news to the poor. He has sent me to bind up the brokenhearted, to proclaim freedom for the captives, and release from darkness for the prisoners, to proclaim the favorable year of the LORD and the day of vengeance of our God; to comfort all who mourn..."*

Jesus came to preach the good news of salvation from sin. What is our response to sin? We humble ourselves before God. We repent and change our direction. We recognize God's way is better, and we choose His way over our own.

Jesus also came to heal the brokenhearted. Brokenhearted doesn't mean "sad," per say. It means that our heart, our soul, is wounded, it is disjointed, it is not whole. It means that there are ruts at our core that have been worn deep by the patterns of our response to wounds. Jesus came to resolve this; He came to heal your fractured soul and mine.

If I say that I don't need Jesus's healing or comfort, am I not like Peter who refused to let Jesus wash his feet? *"If I do not wash you, you have no part with Me."** If I refuse to let Jesus have his way and fulfill His whole mission within me, what am I missing out on?

So many of us trying to address these two issues, sin and wounding, in the same manner. Our frustration grows, however, when we repeatedly try to solve a wounding issue by repenting. What we really need, in that case, is healing.

What behaviors does woundedness generate in our lives? Hiding. Running. Concealing. Minimizing. Habits. There are many traits of woundedness, and God wants to minister to us in them. He wants to bring comfort, acceptance, correction of false perspectives of ourselves and of Him, exchange of the things that caused the brokenness, and unity with Him. In short, He wants to bring healing! The thing is, healing cannot be done through repentance, obligation or duty. We cannot heal ourselves. And, if we attempt to "repent" of our woundedness, it only adds guilt and shame.

## Conclusion

Our ability to live authentically, in our True Identity, is hampered the very first time we are wounded. And, when our authenticity is thwarted, we inevitably develop an inauthentic way of perceiving life, of communicating, and of portraying ourselves. It affects every relationship we have, and it has a powerful effect on how we see and approach God.

When we see God primarily through a filter of inaccurate perspectives, old wounds, incomplete truths, and assumptions, we are limited in how well we can connect with Him. And, if we don't know what authenticity looks like in our own personal life, how in the world are we supposed to be authentic with our Father in heaven?

Life is an epic story; it is *your* story. Your Father, the King, has a birthright awaiting you. He has resources at your beck and call. He has protection for you. He has titles and privilege for you. He has a name for you. He has a mission for you. And you are approaching the point in the story where all these elements will begin to converge. Are you ready? It's "Go" time!

---

* John 13:8

17

# Chapter two
## Prayer: Messages from the King

Jonathan and Jonet walked among the rows of bundled food, as the afternoon sun created long shadows on the field. The two of them could see other children meandering between basket and bushel, browsing for something new that might appeal to them more—more than all the predicable produce that automatically appeared to them each day.

The Fields of Plenty glowed in the waning sunlight of the day, and Jonathan and Jonet's shadows stretched out far beyond them. Jonet happened to drop her gaze to her feet, and curiously she followed the silhouetted form with her eyes all the way to the city wall, where it continued vertically up the wall, with the profile of her head ending abruptly at eye level on the stone facade.

Jonathan turned as well, wondering what was holding Jonet's attention. "Your head looks so small!" he goofed. She giggled and agreed, and they both scampered over to the wall for a closer look, with the hopes that their silly shadows would stay in the same place as they approached the stone wall.

Now the children didn't know the name of the city that this wall encircled. In fact, they tended to forget there was even life behind it. In this way, the wall became its own entity, and in their minds, it could have existed on its own without a civilization behind it. They are, after all, children, and you know how easy it is for youngsters to change their perception of the world by how they imagine it. The fortification began to take on an existence of its own. The children simply called it *the Uppity Wall,* silly as it sounded.

Jonathan and Jonet stood together, facing the Uppity Wall, with their shadows before them. As they admired their silhouettes, the stone between them began to make a funny sound. "Jonet, do you hear that scratchy noise?"

"I do! I do! But I don't see anything. Whatever could it be?"

And slowly, the mortar around the stone began to dust their feet with finely ground powder, then sand-sized particles, and finally, brittle chunks of grout, as it became clear that someone was trying to dig through the wall.

19

When the scraping and crumbling finally quieted down, the two children became aware of a voice on the other side of the massive stones. It was muffled, and distant, and it sounded low and strong—not like the voices of the other children.

"Mmmfftepugh."

Jonathan and Jonet snapped back and looked at each other. "What did it say?" they wondered. Both of them leaned in very close and nestled their ears up against the edge of the stone, as though they might be able to fit their ear in the mortar gap. And the voice spoke again.

"Jonathan. Jonet. Can you hear me???" This time, the question was clear, and the voice sounded concerned.

"Children, do you hear me!" It came again louder this time. Now, the two children were still astounded that there was a voice to begin with—let alone that it knew their names. But they also felt an urgency that overcame their shock. "We do—we can hear you!" they replied.

"Here, take this…" came the voice, as a small, iron object began to make its way between the stones. Whoever was on the other side was pushing it through somehow. The metal object ground and grated between the blocks of stone, and when it finally emerged on their side of the wall and fell into Jonet's hand, they saw the most ornately fashioned key they had ever laid eyes on.

By this time, the other children began to take notice, and were running toward the two.

"What is it, what is it?" asked one.

"Be careful of the Uppity Wall! exclaimed another.

The clamoring voices of the other children made it impossible to hear the distant voice on the other side of the wall. The few, fleeting moments the voice was recognizable had vanished, only to be replaced by cautionary quips and frenzied queries. It was all a bit too much to take in, and so, out of a need to escape the commotion, Jonet quietly slipped the key into her pocket. The other children were unaware of the voice, and they had not noticed the key. It was as if they had been riled up simply at the thought of discovering something curious, without actually discovering it.

Jonathan and Jonet snuck away, far from the other children, and when the coast was clear, they pulled out the key again. Wiping away the grit and dust from the key, a single word appeared along the shaft. It simply said, "Come."

## Reading between the lines

Jonathan and Jonet continue their purposeless existence in a world with limits—barriers that they perceive to be rigid, black-and-white, or perhaps even pretentious and exclusionary. But beyond this seemingly safe boundary, the voice of God beckons to them. It extends an invitation to the both of them—though where it leads is unknown. And scary. And exciting. And validates, in a certain way, that there may just be that "missing" thing out there after all. And, as often is the case, the others in their same predicament issue warnings that are intended to keep them from leaving their safe little world. These voices, unfortunately, can be loud enough to drown out our Father's invitations to us.

## What is your prayer life like?

For most of us, that is a question we'd rather not have to be honest about. "I don't feel close to God when I pray." "My prayers seem to hit the ceiling." "I don't get answers to my prayers." "My prayers feel dead." "I get really distracted when I pray." "It is hard to stay awake when I pray." "God seems distant." "'Whatever you ask in My name, I will do it,' doesn't happen for me."

Am I missing something?

So often, it seems that our prayer just doesn't work. And when it doesn't work, we don't do it as much. There was a time in my life when I completely stopped. Why is this? Could it be that one of the following may apply to you as it did to me? Do you come to God with *your* own agenda? Do you ask God to prosper your plans? Do you try to convince God of the merit of your plan? Do you monologue at Him without stopping to listen to what He has to say? Do you try to create some fervor and yearning in your voice to show God how serious you are? Do you pray "extra-long" to show God that you are persistent?

This isn't really prayer; this is manipulation. And, if you, being human, can recognize manipulation from someone else, how much more so does our Father know when we are trying to butter him up for a favorable response?

I remember feeling a pressure, for most of my Christian life, to pray good prayers. I think many of us have that one grandpa that prays in old "King James" English. Do "thee's" and "thou's" make it a holier prayer? I learned to pray verbose prayers, prayers that sounded like an orator had crafted them. They were spectacular verbal achievements, I was sure, but I also knew that I was inwardly just hoping to impress God. This was my goal for so many years, because I didn't really know Him, how to pray, or how to understand what He wanted in the process. As I came to find out, prayer is very natural, and the best prayer is honest prayer—prayer that marries what is going on in our mind with what is going on in our gut, and presents it as a singular, harmonious thought to the Father. Let's give ourselves the freedom to speak naturally with Him, and stop all the rhetoric, the fancy words, the theological sermons in prayer, and please oh please, all the repetitious words, like *Father God*, like *just*, and *somehow*. "Father God, would You just, somehow, Father God, just help us, Father God, to just, just somehow love You more, Father God."

Who is it exactly that we pray to? Do we pray to Jesus? Do we pray to the Father? Do we pray to the Holy Spirit? If we take Jesus's words literally, that He is the only way to the Father, then prayer naturally begins with Jesus; before we can know the Father, we must know the Son. For many of us, Jesus is the person we normally pray to. The Father however, doesn't get as much mention, perhaps because He feels more distant to us. Jesus plays the central role in our theology, and there is a certain safety that we feel when praying to Him. Some people pray to the Holy Spirit, but for a vast majority of others, this idea seems uncertain and we wonder if perhaps it may be wrong to pray to the Holy Spirit.

If we can learn from Jesus's example, we observe that He consistently checks in with the Father. Even in John 17, Jesus tells his disciples that He will pray to the Father so that He will send the Holy Spirit. If Jesus makes Himself the doorway through which we access the Father through salvation, and if the ministry of the Holy Spirit is all about drawing people back to the Father, then it is safe to assume that the Father is who Jesus and the Holy Spirit both want us to pray to.

There is a sort of evolution in how we pray. It begins as the Holy Spirit draws us on behalf of the Father.[*] The Holy Spirit gives us life as He activates our spirits, and He gets the wheels turning, so to speak.[†] Once our journey toward the Father gets underway, we are brought to Jesus: He is both our attorney[‡] and our judge.[§] He is the one who holds the authority to justify us and give us permission to approach the Father. And, as He said, "No one comes to the Father except through Me."[**] This now becomes the main emphasis of our spiritual journey: oneness with the Father. He works to draw us to Himself, and to reveal Himself as our Abba, our Papa,[††] and He showers us with honor and affection[‡‡] along the way.

The Holy Spirit is the flow that pulls us toward Jesus Christ, so that we may receive salvation and all the wonderful privilege of brotherhood with the Son. And, the Holy Spirit remains the flow that pulls us through that threshold of salvation, that spiritual checkpoint that is Jesus, and forward into the arms of the

---

[*] John 6:44
[†] John 6:63, Romans 8:10
[‡] 1 Timothy 2:5, 1 John 2:1
[§] John 5:27
[**] John 14:6
[††] Romans 8:15, Galatians 4:6
[‡‡] Ephesians 1:5-6

Father. Jesus is all about authority, the Holy Spirit is all about Access, and the Father is all about Affection.

Christians often have such apprehension about the Father that we are timid to come to Him. When we read passages that encourage us to boldly approach the throne of grace, we often forget the theme of Ephesians, that our Father has kind affection toward us. Approaching Him boldly has nothing to do with how cleaned up we are or how diligent we have been. Instead, it has everything to do with the fact that He dreamed us up, He brought us to life, He pulled us toward Himself, and He wants to reveal us to His Creation like the beaming father He is.*

## What exactly is prayer?

Conceptually, prayer is the forum where we have exchanges with God. Prayer is the vehicle through which we experience the Holy Spirit, our role in the Body of Christ, our spiritual gifting, Divine Authority, Divine Power, Calling, Identity, spiritual warfare, etc.

Prayer is not just a monologue from us to God. Prayer is alive! Prayer is our real-time dialogue with our Father who is just on the other side of the veil. Prayer is the exchange where we pour out to our Father and He responds to us. Prayer is the exchange where God calls us to Himself, and we respond to Him.

Prayer is the place we experience deep intimacy with our Abba, our Father. However, prayer is also the venue where we experience deep connection and unity with our brothers and sisters in the Body of Christ. Just like the apostles who were gathered in one accord, when we come together as a family and ask our Father what His agenda is, and we collectively join Him in it, the Holy Spirit empowers and connects and employs His children for His supernatural purpose. This is not speculation, nor is it simply a theology. This is real, and it is a regular occurrence for the children of God who practice it.

Has your prayer life delivered these results?

Practically speaking, prayer is the act of our spirit communing with God's Spirit. The Scriptures teach us that our spirit is brought to life the moment we first surrender ourselves to Jesus Christ,† and as a result, the Holy Spirit lives inside each child of God,‡ the Spirit speaks to us,§ and we can remain in a constant state of communication with the Spirit of God.**

---

* Romans 8:16-19
† See Romans 8
‡ 1 Corinthians 3:16
§ 1 Corinthians 2:12-13
** Ephesians 6:18

This is what John 15 calls *abiding*, and what John 17 calls *oneness*.

Abiding implies a constancy. If we only look at this in a physical sense, it can seem overwhelming. *"Constantly in a state of prayer? But I have to go to work!"* When we instead look at this state of connectedness with God from the perspective of our spirit, it begins to gain a little more traction. If we *are* spirit, newly brought to life in Christ, and our spirit is in a state of union with the Holy Spirit, then it really doesn't matter what arbitrary activity of everyday life we are involved in; all of life is spiritual. Going to work is a spiritual act. Travel is a spiritual act. Eating is a spiritual act. Socializing is a spiritual act. Sitting on the freeway can be the most spiritual encounter you have with God the whole day. What about the night hours? Our spirit doesn't sleep. I think this is why the Father beckons His children to pray, to talk with Him, during the stillness of the night; our spirits are unencumbered by our minds and bodies that are deep in rest.

Prayer is the act of rejoining the unending conversation between our spirit and the Holy Spirit. Our spirit is an ally of God, as it owes its life to Him. As such, our spirit is the part of us that most easily connects with God. Our spirit, if healthy, maintains this ongoing connection with the Holy Spirit, even when we are unaware of it! This connection with God does not require spoken words, but it does require honesty.

With this in mind, effective prayer involves our listening as the Holy Spirit speaks, as well as our response as He invites. Effective prayer requires that we say "Yes!" to Him: agreeing with Him, and joining Him where He leads. Effective prayer, therefore, requires that we yield our agendas to Him, deferring to His purpose and His desire. Effective prayer, then, could be described as the conscious choice to align with God.

## Aligning with the Father

*"Truly, truly, I say to you, he who believes in Me, the works that I do, he will do also; and greater works than these he will do; because I go to the Father. Whatever you ask in My name, that will I do, so that the Father may be glorified in the Son. If you ask Me anything in My name, I will do it."* John 14:12-14

Now, just to clarify, "in Jesus's name" does not make His name a magical formula. Some would take this scripture to mean that all we have to do is say "in Jesus's name" and poof! our prayers are answered. In the Greek, "name" can certainly mean exactly that—a name, but the other meaning of the word is "cause, interests, etc." In other words, *"Whatever you ask in My interest, that will I do..."*

How do we know what His interest is?

We discover His interests in prayer, as we listen to His voice through the Holy Spirit. His prompting is real-time. His guidance is real-time. His conviction is real-time. His interest is, therefore, communicated in real-time as well. When we pray in agreement with His interests as He reveals them to us, His response is always "Yes!"

This was precisely what the Son modeled for us during His time as a human being.

Many scholars and theologians throughout the centuries have examined how Jesus prayed. Some have formed theology around their findings. Others have formed acronyms to help us remember elements of His prayers. I believe that if we remember the most basic element of Jesus's prayers, the rest will be intuitive.

Jesus yielded His will to the Father's, in every prayer that we see in the Scriptures.

*"Our Father, who is in Heaven, Hallowed be Your name. Your kingdom come, Your will be done..."* Matthew 6:9-10

*"Oh My Father, if it is possible, let this cup pass from Me; yet not as I will, but as You will."* Matthew 26:39

Between Jesus's statements of yielding to the Father are other elements: His needs and desires, His worship and gratitude. But, the singular pattern is that He always brings Himself into a state of yieldedness the Father. As a result of Jesus remaining yielded to the Father's agenda, and remaining in a state of abiding with the Holy Spirit, He was filled with the power of God as each moment of His Father's mission required. This, then, is the context of His words to us, *"If you ask anything in My name, I will do it."*

Jesus first modeled the very lifestyle He promised to us.

## Hearing God

The idea that a human being can hear the voice of God instantly wells up fear and skepticism for many Christians. There is so much baggage wrapped up in this concept.

Many Christians resist this idea because of how they process the implications of saying we can hear God's voice. I know this first-hand, because I felt exactly the same way. I can appreciate all of the objections that are raised. But, I hope to set your mind at ease as we address these hangups.

Hearing the voice of God does not mean that you are holier than other people. It does not guarantee that you won't act like an idiot.[*] It does not mean that you

---

[*] Galatians 2:11-14

won't choose to sin.[*] It does not ensure that you will grow spiritually.[†] In short, hearing God's voice does not make you more "special" than other people.

So why is it that we fear hearing God? There are lots of reasons why we fear: He may be displeased with us, His tone may be harsh, we may hear Him "wrong," He may not answer, others may judge us, He may tell us to do something we don't want to do, and hearing Him may take us into territory where we don't want to go. Many Christians fear they are simply not spiritual enough to hear Him.

The reality of Scripture is that God is shown speaking, many times, to people in the midst of their process of sinning. God engages with Cain during his progression of murder,[‡] with Jonah in his disobedience,[§] with Balaam during his betrayal of Israel,[**] and who can forget Judas as he plotted to betray Jesus?[††]

Furthermore, God is shown speaking with several characters in the Scriptures who are not even of the children of Israel. God speaks to Laban,[‡‡] Hagar,[§§] and Cornelius,[***] and He speaks to *and through* the pagan kings Nebuchadnezzar,[†††] Abimelech,[‡‡‡] and Cyrus,[§§§] among others.

So, the fear that we are not spiritual enough is not a valid argument based on how God communicates in the Scriptures.

For those that fear the Father will be condemning, we need to take a fresh look at John 5 where we are told that "not even the Father judges anyone, but He has given all judgment to the Son...and He gave Him authority to execute judgment." The Father has equipped Jesus Christ to be the gatekeeper, so to speak, leaving the Father free for affection toward His children. I don't mean to oversimplify this concept, but it has proven consistently true in our experience in ministry.

---

[*] Hebrews 6
[†] 2 Timothy 4:10
[‡] Genesis 4
[§] Jonah 4
[**] Numbers 22
[††] Luke 22
[‡‡] Genesis 31
[§§] Genesis 21:14-20
[***] Acts 10
[†††] Daniel 2
[‡‡‡] Genesis 20:1-7
[§§§] Ezra 1:1-4

26

# What does it mean to "hear God?"

I realize that this can be a misunderstood notion, so let's look at some truths associated with hearing God.

First, we need to recognize that God has been speaking to us all along, and we have simply attributed it to something else. God speaks to us by: inspiring thoughts in our minds,[*] prompting us to take action,[†] and giving us messages for others, or them for us.[‡]

Second, we need to understand that God illustrates messages to us using language, imagery, sounds, emotions, etc., that we "get." God speaks both boldly[§] and calmly.[**] He calls us to action using casual directives[††] and strong imperatives.[‡‡] He shows us concepts in mental pictures and in dreams.[§§] He "feeds" us words to say in moments of ministry.[***]

Desiree recognizes the Father's communication as something she "hears," not audibly, but within her heart. For me, He speaks in pictures, even when it is a "yes" or "no" answer; I will actually see a picture of the word in my heart. The same goes for how we perceive the presence of God; some feel it, some hear it, but I get pictures of how His presence is manifesting.

I can certainly appreciate that the variety of descriptions here may be difficult for some to consider. After all, should God be more consistent in how He communicates? If He really wants to commune with people, why does He make it so hard to figure out?

I think of our three children; all three communicate differently by design. Two are introverts, and one is an extrovert. One is boisterous, one is quite reserved, and one is in between. All three have varying levels of emotional expression. One is an auditory learner, one a tactile learner, and one a visual learner. One needs to have the message be blunt and direct, while another responds best to an indirect approach. Furthermore, all three represent varying levels of maturity. When Desiree and I want to communicate something significant to them, we try to be deliberate in how we get their attention and how we convey the message. It looks

---

[*] Acts 10:19
[†] Acts 8:29, 11:12
[‡] Acts 11:28, 13:2
[§] Job 40:6
[**] 1 Kings 19:11-12
[††] Acts 13:4
[‡‡] Acts 16:6
[§§] Acts 10
[***] John 14:26

different from one child to the other. I believe our heavenly Father does the same for us, and just like we have to adapt our communication style with our children as they mature and their processing skills improve, I believe our Father knows how He designed each of us and adapts His communication accordingly.

When our Father speaks to us, His love dissolves and resolves our fears.[*] Sometimes He communicates His love toward us according to our love language, the specific way we most easily understand love. He starts small at first, showing us just as much love as we can handle, and He continues to reveal more and more love toward us as we grow with Him. This is *Intimacy* with the Father, and living this way is *Abiding*. It leads us down the path of discovery that we are His beloved!

In this process of learning, we encounter the truth that His leading will never contradict Scripture. As we get to know His voice, we learn to validate and to trust His promptings. We learn to look for our Father at work, anytime, anywhere. When thoughts cross our mind during prayer, we ask Him if He is trying to communicate something. We ask Him if "random" occurrences are actually specific blessings. We cultivate our tuning by accepting His invitations, and we actively pursue confirmation in Scripture.

As we learn to abide in Him, He leads us into deep spiritual renovation. And, in the process, we get to know Him better, we receive epiphanies from Him about His design for us, and we discover our true identity is that we are His Beloved.


## Conclusion

The truth of the matter is that *hearing God* was His intent from the very beginning. The Bible opens with Adam and Eve, Cain, Esau, and the Patriarchs, hearing God and having one on one communication with Him.

Then, at a fateful moment in history, the children of Israel interrupted the flow of this communication with a choice that they made. Exodus 19 and 20 chronicle the following excerpt:

God extends a promise to the children of Israel, *"...If you will indeed obey My voice and keep My covenant, then you shall be My own possession among all the peoples, for all the earth is Mine; and you shall be to Me a kingdom of priests and a holy nation."*

The people respond positively and promise to keep God's covenant. God then tells Moses, "Behold, I will come to you in a thick cloud, so that the people may hear when I speak..."

---

[*] 1 John 4:18

However, when the people saw the lightning and heard the thunder, they were afraid and stood far away, and told Moses, "Speak to us yourself and we will listen; but let not God speak to us, or we will die."

Moses tries to convince the people that there is nothing to fear, that this was just God's way of showing His magnitude, but the people refused to engage with God. And, in my opinion, this pivotal moment was representative of the Israelites' attitude toward God, and as a result, their collective desire to not have to engage with God was honored by Him. From that point on, it seems that the potential "kingdom of priests" was reduced to a handful of priests speaking to God on behalf of the majority of the people.

And then Jesus came and restored access to the Father to all His children once again, this time facilitated by the Holy Spirit living within us.

# Chapter three

## Your Backstory: False Self emerges

Jonathan and Jonet were just children. All they had known was the immediacy of their wants and needs. Exhaustion. Hunger. Thirst. But now, a puzzling new desire was beginning to emerge, and it had to do with the voice. It seemed as though the one it belonged to *knew* the children.

"How did he know our names?" "Who was that man?" And of course, their curiosity kept the question of the key at the forefront of conversation. What would it open? There were no locks on any doors in Freeman's Forest, but each child did have a treasure chest where they kept anything of value. This key, however, was far too grand to fit any of those minuscule locks.

"Come." The invitation that was embossed upon the key occupied their young minds increasingly. "Come where?" And, as young children are prone to do, they imagined countless scenarios between the two of them as to the function of the key.

What they finally decided was that—since the key came from the Uppity Wall— that must be where they were invited to go. And so, determination in their steps, they made their way to the wall. They took the long way through the forest in order to avoid the other children and any questions that might come up. And they certainly didn't want to take the risk of anyone else taking the key from them. After all, the key was given to *them* by name. *It was theirs*.

Jonet and Jonathan wandered the perimeter of the wall, looking for something out of the ordinary—anything that would give them a clue to the purpose of the key. They pushed on any stone in the wall that looked unusual. And into any little crevice they encountered, the key was thrust, but to no avail. By this point, Jonathan and Jonet's curiosity had turned to desire; and desire to longing; and longing to obsession. For the first time in their memory, the two children were experiencing a need that was stronger than food, and more penetrating than rest. Obsession—in its fruitless search along the Uppity Wall—began to give way to desperation.

"We are never going to find where this key fits!" exclaimed Jonet, partly yelling, and partly choking back tears of frustration.

Their faces grimy with sweat and smears of dirt, the weary children slumped to the ground. And there, among the tall grasses at the base of the wall, they slept.

"Jonathan. Jonet. Come!"

The two children sat up with a start and looked square in each other's eyes. The voice was unmistakable. It seemed so close! Groggy from sleep, and still on their hands and knees, they spun to and fro, looking for the voice. The wall was solid. The sky was vacant. But just then, just a few steps away from where they slept, they noticed something that didn't belong. They scrambled over to it—on hands and feet, as only youngsters can do—and took a closer look. Embedded within the thatch of the deep grass was something wooden, and with a flurry of energy, Jonathan and Jonet cleared all of the debris off the top of it.

"It's a trap door!"

"It has a key hole!"

And quicker than a blink, Jonet had pulled the key out and stuck it deep into the lock. With a flick of the wrist, the key turned. There was no hesitation on her part. And there was no question of fitment of the key. The trap door was unlocked with one fluid movement. As soon as the lock was unlatched, the door sprung open—as if the lock was only meant to hold the door closed.

Jonathan peered down into the opening. There were steps that made their way down and underneath the wall. Still up on top of the grass, he lay down flat and peeked his head down into the hole. His eyes followed the stone steps downward to a stone floor. The cobbled floor matched the walls, and he could also make out torches—unlit—upon the walls. He couldn't see the end of this space, but he was pretty sure it was a passage, not a room. And as he lay there, trying to adjust his eyes to the low light of the passage, he began to hear faint sounds coming from the far end of the passage. He figured that the subterranean hallway must be quite long, based on the dim light and distant noise.

The duo sat up and looked at each other. Neither of them spoke. But it was clear that they were considering what lay before them. Minutes passed—and the instinctual movement that had pulled the key and opened the trap door with seamless fluidity had been replaced by the paralysis of uncertainty. What lay beyond? Who was the voice? Why did he know their names? Would they be cold or hungry? Would danger await?

And so, exchanging glances with each other, Jonathan reached up, grabbed the top of the trap door, and lowered it until it was shut. Jonet turned the key clockwise to lock it. It was slightly more difficult to turn the key to lock it again—as though it didn't want to be locked.

The two of them rose to their feet, and instinctively walked back across the Fields of Plenty, deep into Freeman's Forest where they plodded along the well-worn tracks that they could navigate with eyes closed. It was back to their ordinary world.

## Reading between the lines

Jonathan and Jonet—Christians in theory only—have been called, by name, by God. Perhaps they do not yet know who the voice belongs to, but maybe there is a spark deep inside that has identified exactly who it is. And with this knowledge, their souls sense the resolution to all that has been missing. But as they find out precisely where and how to unlock access to God with His key, a fear sets in. What will He be like? How will He treat me? Will He be disappointed in me?

## Your Backstory

Every hero has a backstory. It is our backstory that is formative to our destiny. Our backstory sets the stage for the conflict—the breakthrough, that influences our Calling.

In the case of the Apostle Paul, his backstory involved great positional authority in the religious system. He was a great achiever; He did things on God's behalf. And, as we recall from the book of Acts, his action was based out of his assumptions about God.

And then, one day, Saul, as he was formerly known, had an encounter with God. He experienced God in the exact way that he needed to. He was knocked to the ground, off of his high horse (pun intended), and was flattened. He was blinded for a season. When Paul finally emerged from his seclusion, He knew God. He obeyed as God directed him. His action was based out of his transforming encounter with God. And as a result, he had zero *positional* authority remaining, but incredible *spiritual* authority.

In the case of the woman in Luke 7, she had lived a lifestyle that was devoted to sin. She had a reputation as an immoral woman, and she was scorned by the religious leadership.

And then, one day, this woman had an encounter with God. She approached Jesus in her shame, and showed great faith in doing so. She scandalously and conspicuously lavished her tears and perfume upon Him. And, as a result, Jesus immortalized her faith in the Scriptures and forgave her.

Your backstory is significant. It is significant because of what you have experienced. It is significant because of what you have *not* experienced. Both Saul/Paul and the woman in Luke 7 have backstories that greatly affected how they approached life. Both of them viewed the world, viewed themselves, and viewed God through the filter of what they had lived thus far.

What about you? What is your backstory?

## Your False Self

Each one of us has been influenced by our environment, our relationships, and our peers, and this influence has encrusted over the authentic identity our Father designed in us. When we live disconnected from our authentic self, we begin to develop, increasingly, a false perspective of ourselves, of the world, and of God, that can ultimately consume us; this is the genesis of our False Self.

Our False Self is first triggered by the wounds of everyday life, and life is certainly full of them. Some wounds are big, and some are small. Some are deeply significant, and some are much less impactful. Some are a one-time occurrence, and some are part of a recurring cycle. Some wounds are born out of trauma, while some wounds result from good intentions.

Wounds naturally open the door to lies. We get hurt, and a message is delivered: "You are unlovable," "You can't depend on anyone else," etc. These lies become recurring themes throughout our lives, and we ultimately end up living in agreement with or in reaction against these lies. Either way, these messages maintain a control over us and become the filter that we operate through. Lies can also come from other sources than wounds. Lies can come straight from the enemy of our souls, as well as the world around us: popular culture, television and magazines.

Lies spark a visceral reaction within us: either agreement or denial. And both of these reactions lead us to create vows. "I *am* a failure—I will never amount to *anything*." Or perhaps, "I will *never* be like that!" When we live out these vows, they become the catalyst for much of what we do and don't do. Vows can be difficult to identify in our lives, when compared with lies that seem to constantly be at the forefront of our minds.

Finally, the repetitive action that comes out of those vows slowly builds a barrier around us. Perhaps the barrier is a facade, intended to persuade ourselves and others of some identity we have associated with. The barrier can also be a wall, keeping loved ones and relationships at a distance.

These four stages, Wounds, Lies, Vows, and Facades, are what our False Self is made of. We are all affected by this False Self, to some extent or another. It is this False Self that robs us of our destiny by keeping us blinded to our True Identity.

Because of this, our Father is deeply committed to revealing this to us. He will go to any length necessary to expose our False Self so that we can be freed from it, and released into the abundance He created for us.

Until this reckoning occurs, you and I are posers. We project who we want to be seen as. We aspire to be like others. We pine away for the kind of intimacy with God that we see in our *heroes of the faith*. We exhaust ourselves "doing" for God. We exalt theology over prayer. And tragically, we miss the point of knowing God.

When False Self is our filter, everything we observe and encounter is interpreted through it. We certainly see ourselves through that skewed perspective. But, we also view others and process relationships through the lies and the noise of our False Self. And, our understanding of God, of our Father, is perhaps most precariously impacted by the warped lenses we wear. We end up defining God, even choosing certain theology, in compliance with our messed-up points of view.

## False Self as our Filter

When we view ourselves through the eyes of our False Self, there are several ways that our self-perception can be skewed. We can latch onto a defeatist mantra, claiming that we were born inferior due to: a learning disability, atypical appearance, or unique disposition. We may hone in on what we see as character flaws: "I am inadequate," "I am a failure," "I am unworthy." Perhaps we can only see as far as certain developed traits: "I am lazy," "I am a quitter," "I am defiled," or even, "I am an achiever." And finally, we can even become so tunnel-visioned that we only see ourselves through certain associations: "I am a victim," "I am an addict," "I am a control-freak," and perhaps, "I am an alpha-male." It is important to note that *positive* distortions can be just as much of a trap as *negative* ones!

You have probably heard it said, *"If you lie to yourself long enough, you will eventually believe it."* This is so true! And likewise, if we listen to the lies of the enemy, we can be robbed of the destiny God has for us. I recognize that there are many Christians who would assert that if God has plans, they will come to pass, no matter what. Therefore, if He destined us for something, it will happen because He is sovereign. To this, I would simply reply that there are several instances throughout the Gospels where the disciples had opportunity to participate in a supernatural display of God's power, but they could not, because of their unbelief. If their unbelief could interrupt what God was prepared to perform, doesn't 'at the same hold true for us? If we disbelieve the truth of who God says we are and what He equipped us specially to do, it stands to reason that we will miss out on it, just like the disciples did.

When we engage in relationship with others in the shell of our False Self, it is nearly impossible to find true intimacy, since intimacy is based in authenticity and honesty. How can we be intimate when we are trying to be genuine through the distortions of our facade? False Self can manifest in different ways in a relationship. We "hold back" from our spouse and family. We can be hyper-sensitive to the slightest perceived offense. We can be surrounded by people, but feel completely alone. Accountability groups fail. Friendships stall out. And, ultimately, we only know how to reveal certain aspects of our self.

Our False Self approaches authenticity this way: "I'm just keeping it real!" "That's just who I am...if you don't like it, I guess we can't be friends." It can end up abusing "honesty" by feeling justified in verbally unleashing on someone else, all in the name of "being true to yourself." The perceived authenticity of False Self is harmful, demeaning, and isolating, and is extremely unhealthy.

And then, there is ministry. This one hits close to home for me, as I spent many years "hiding out" in ministry. Some people stray and wander from the flock; I decided to double my efforts and feed my False Self by serving in just about any capacity the church had need of. Perhaps most poignant to me now is the time I spent as a "worship leader." I knew nothing of actual worship, yet I was in a position of authority and influence.

False Self in ministry is the single biggest reason for mediocrity in the Church today. What does it look like? Perhaps I insert myself as the solution to a ministry need without any direction from the Father. I am simply a body in a role. I have no burden or longing for the people. It could be that I have no passion for the need. I have no instruction from God to fill this role. And, as a result, I am my own power source and motivation.

There are a few possible outcomes.

**Positive**: I may accidentally find myself in alignment with God's will—where He actually is actively at work, and by happy coincidence, my efforts happen to make a positive contribution.

**Neutral**: My volunteering helps meet a physical need, but since I am not responding to God's invitation, but choosing my own path, He is not empowering the work. In other words, "It's a good thing, but not a God thing."

**Negative**: I could actually be filling a role intended for someone else, and as a result, I am impeding the will of God by working contrary to His purposes. This is the exact position Simon Peter found himself in when, in his zeal, chided Jesus for saying that He came to die. Peter was going to fight for Him. Peter was zealous for God. But, Jesus rebuked him with those famous words, *"Get behind Me, adversary! You are a stumbling block to Me; for you are not setting your mind of God's interests, but man's!"*[*]

It is deeply sobering to consider that we may be interfering in God's work. Not every moment is ours to step into. Not every opportunity is ours to assert ourselves

---

[*] Matthew 16:23

on God's behalf. One such moment in the life of Jesus occurs in John 2:4, at the wedding in Cana, when Mary, Jesus's mother, asks Him to do something about the shortage of wine for the guests. His response was, *"Woman, what does this have to do with us? My hour has not yet come."* Paul encounters a similar moment in Acts 16:6-7:

*"They passed through the Phrygian and Galatian region, having been forbidden by the Holy Spirit to speak the word in Asia; and after they came to Mysia, they were trying to go into Bithynia, and the Spirit of Jesus did not permit them..."*

In any type of ministry, we must remain in tune with the voice of the Holy Spirit in our hearts; it is how we remain aligned with the will of the Father. And when we are aligned with Him, He brings fruitfulness and fulfillment. I love how A.W. Tozer puts it:

*"The Church is languishing for leaders, but for the right kind of leaders; for the wrong kind is worse than none at all. Better to stand still than to follow a blind man over a precipice...The ideal leader is one who hears the voice of God and beckons the people on as the voice calls him and them."*[*]

In ministry, then, it comes down to listening to our own voice (or the voice of the enemy), or listening to God's voice. Our False Self listens to its own perspectives and it listens to the lies that have influenced us for so long. Our Authentic Self listens to the voice of God and chooses His will, His purpose, His agenda.

In other words, it is the difference between *doing things right* and *doing the right things.*

False Self is good at *doing things right.* This is performance-based Christianity. This is the mode where we maintain a good image on the outside. We do for God. We buckle down. We exhaust ourselves in our duty. There is no rest, and there is no vitality. And, whether we succeed or fail, as we define those terms, the only outcome can be pride. It is pride when we beam in our "success," and it is also pride when we wallow in our "failure." Our pride dictates that we can do something to improve our standing with God or to diminish it.

Authentic Self is concerned with *doing the right things.* This is based entirely in our response to God's promptings on a small scale, and our response to His Calling on a grand scale. *Doing the right things* is how we live out our True Identity. It is energizing. It is fulfilling. We get to rest in between His promptings, as He is not intent on burning us out. Our appearance is only a by-product, and the further we proceed into this immersion with God, the less we are concerned about how we are perceived. How do we know what *the right things* are? In this

---

[*] The Warfare of the Spirit, Chapter 41, Leaders and Followers. A.W. Tozer Wingspread Publishers, 2006

context, *the right things* are the invitations and promptings we hear from God. If we don't listen, we cannot hear them.

## When Facades become Barriers

What is your facade? One of my facades was being a "tough guy." I wanted so badly to be respected and to be taken seriously in my youth. I didn't want to be pushed around by bullies any longer. My goal was for other men to recognize me as a force to be reckoned with. My dad, a career police officer, had made it clear that he didn't want me to experience the dangerous and difficult life of law enforcement, so it was up to me to come up with a different method to earn that "tough as nails" image. I listened to a specific kind of music, dressed a particular way, walked with a swagger, and so on. But it was all pretense. Underneath it all, I knew that I was a poser; *we all are*. It is different for everyone: peacemaker, star pupil, victim, strong independent woman, addict, sports enthusiast, biker, rebel, etc. What is one of *your* facades?

These facades, and countless others, serve to protect our hearts; they are defenses that we have developed in response to our woundedness. And, as Brennan Manning portrays it in *Abba's Child*, False Self was how we survived, and it is a necessary part of our backstory.

But, we all come to the point where these facades become barriers. What was originally intended to be a protective castle has become an isolating prison. These barriers separate us from connection with God, with others, and even with our Authentic Self.

This is nothing new. In fact, we can trace this brokenness all the way back to the Garden of Eden in Genesis 3, as five specific barriers were introduced to humanity: Doubt, Knowing, Authority and Approval, Responsibility, and Hiding. Can you spot them in the story?

*"Now the serpent was more crafty than any beast of the field which the LORD God had made. And he said to the woman, 'Indeed, has God said, 'You shall not eat from any tree of the garden'? The woman said to the serpent, 'From the fruit of the trees of the garden we may eat; but from the fruit of the tree which is in the middle of the garden, God has said, 'You shall not eat from it or touch it, or you will die.'' The serpent said to the woman, 'You surely will not die!'"* Genesis 3:1-4

**Doubt**: *"You will not certainly die!"* Doubt is questioning what God says. When Doubt becomes a barrier, our whole foundation is unsettled. Who do we trust? Who can be trusted? Wavering, fear, and apprehension become an overriding influence over us.

**Knowing**: *"Your eyes will be opened, and you will be like God, knowing good and evil."* Knowing is the transition from authentic perspective into a perspective that is based on our own experiences: good, bad, or otherwise. That is why there is such a disconnection between what we intellectually know about God and what we know about Him from experience.

**Authority and Approval**: *"She also gave some to her husband, who was with her, and he ate it."* The barrier of Approval and Authority is based on who we receive our validation from, where we look for it, and what authority we allow to speak into our life. Before the Fall, our only authority was God and the only Being from whom we sought approval was God. If we don't look to Him, we will need to look to someone. This can be especially difficult during our childhood and adolescence, when parental figures hold a significant authority over us. Oftentimes, the greatest damage comes from this source of authority and approval, and based on our own limited experience and understanding at this stage, it is nearly impossible to recognize and defer to God as our greater authority and approval.

**Responsibility**: *"The woman whom You gave to be with me, she gave me of the tree, and I ate."* This barrier influences who we defer responsibility to, and how accountable we hold ourselves. Do we take responsibility for our own action, or do we look to place blame everywhere else possible? What is our part in the matter, and who are we listening to? When it comes to other people's responsibilities, we should consider a few basic questions: *"What is the other person's part? Am I taking on burdens, power, and authority that don't belong to me?"* And subsequently, *"Am I giving over burdens, power, and authority that don't belong to me?"* Finally, God has His own realm of responsibility. *"What is God's part in the matter? Am I trying to take on what belongs to God?"* It can be difficult to make sense of responsibility lines when we are deeply entangled, and we may need God to define proper boundaries for us when they are confused.

**Hiding**: "And they heard the sound of the LORD God walking in the garden in the cool of the day, and Adam and his wife hid themselves from the presence of the LORD God among the trees of the garden."

Hiding is something we all do in our own way. We hide in order to protect our heart. When we hide from God, who contains what we need for wholeness, we will find other ways to avoid the real issue, soothe the shame, cope with the pain, and so on. We seek to hide in "healthy" ways, like exercise, ministry, leadership, and in serving others. And, of course, we hide in "unhealthy" ways as well, like busy-ness, addictive behaviors, self-sufficiency, and hyper-dependence on others.

## Exchanging Barriers

Once we recognize these barriers surrounding us, we can begin to pursue their exchange; the voluntary relinquishment of them in return for something better.

What is that *something better*? It is the very thing that we missed out on from God in the first place. How do we do this? It happens through *reconciliation.*

Reconciliation is the process by which two things that are at odds are brought back into compatibility. In other words, reconciliation is an exchange process that leads to harmony and oneness between our perspective and God's perspective. When the Scriptures speak of reconciliation, we tend to view it strictly through a theological lens, applying to salvation specifically. But, it is really a much grander thing than salvation alone, which is incredible in and of itself. It is grander because it encompasses *all* the aspects of Jesus's mission from Luke 4 and Isaiah 61, including healing.

How does this kind of reconciliation, or spiritual healing, take place?

While I do not like spiritual "formulas," there is a clear pattern that I see over and over again in inner healing. It begins with Identifying our perspective, then Recognizing God's perspective, Clarifying the difference between the two (which reveals what we missed out on), Exchanging our perspective for God's, and finally, the most significant part, Receiving a filling of God's love in what we were missing all along.

Identifying + Recognizing + Clarifying + Exchanging + Receiving = Healing

Where traditional counseling can fall short, and where our own introspection fails to push through, is at the end of the fourth stage: Exchanging. So often, we go through the heartbreak, pain and struggle of this process, make it all the way to Exchanging, which is an intellectual exercise, and we stop there. We start "telling ourselves the truth." This is good, and this is progress, but it is not healing. Spiritual healing is entirely dependent on the last stage, which is Receiving. It is not enough to simply acknowledge the truth; the truth must replace the lies in a supernatural way if it is to have a supernatural result.

Receiving—the part of the process where we are able to just sit quietly with our Father and allow Him to minister to us, through His Holy Spirit—is where we are transformed. It is the process where He pours into us what we were missing out on in the first place. It is the place where "addictions" are resolved, where approval is finalized, and where His authentic design for us is revealed and accepted. This is how intimacy with God takes huge leaps inward.

When we receive what God knows we need, our Doubt is replaced by Trust in Him; our Knowing is replaced by Understanding and Believing His perspective; previous sources of Authority and Approval are replaced by our Father's Authority and Approval over us; old Responsibility lines are replaced by new Recognition of where responsibility lies, and finally, old ways of Hiding are replaced by now Hiding in Him.

## Conclusion

False Self begins as a defense mechanism, or perhaps more accurately, a long series of defense mechanisms, as a way to protect ourselves. But, it inevitably turns into a prison that isolates us from others, from God, from our Authentic Self, and from our destiny.

Such introspection is often considered excessive, or even self-centered by other people who are unhealthy themselves. But, to God, this process of reconciliation, of exchanging our False Self (the old man), with our Authentic Self (the new man), was important enough to make it part of Jesus's mission.

# Chapter four

## Yielding: The Hero is emancipated

Over the next days and weeks, Jonathan and Jonet would pass by the portion of the wall where they had discovered the hatch. They didn't talk about it—they simply cast their glances in the direction of the trap door—nonchalantly, and tried their best to feign disinterest. But deep down, a few things were true: they wanted to confirm that there really was a trap door that would lead them out of the doldrums; that it was still there and the opportunity had not evaded them; and finally, to make sure that no one else had seized upon *their* special discovery.

It was almost one month to the day of the great find that, upon their daily pass by the hatch, Jonathan and Jonet stopped dead in their tracks. She grabbed his arm and clutched it tightly—not out of fear exactly, but rather *alarm*. For there, in their periphery, the wooden lid to the hatch stood conspicuously open. Their hearts raced.

And with a quick glance about them, the two ran over to the hatch; and barely looking inside it, they locked it down as quickly as they could and brushed the surrounding thatch back over the lid. No one could find out about their secret. I didn't even cross their young minds that someone had come through from the other side of the wall.

Confident that they had caught the open hatch in time before any other children could find it, they scurried off. And as the urgency of the moment began to wear off, the children slowed down the pace of their footsteps, and found themselves strolling along the edge of Freeman's Forest.

There, under the shade of the towering Oaks and overlooking the Fields of Plenty, Jonathan spotted another child, kneeling down and resting on the layer of leaves and acorns below. Her eyes were closed, and she didn't seem to take much notice of the two approaching youngsters. As Jonet and Jonathan approached her, she seemed to them quite familiar, but they knew they had not met her before. Perhaps she lived deeper in Freeman's Forest?

"Hello!" called Jonathan.

"Why hello," she replied.

"What's your name?" continued the boy.

"I am Donatella*—and who are you?"

"I am Jonathan, and this is my friend, Jonet." And with these words, Donatella's eyes lit up, and she went from very calm to visibly energized. Jonet noticed the change in her demeanor and concluded she must be quite happy to have met them, which of course, must mean she is a very nice person.

"Jonathan and Jonet, it is so wonderful to meet you!" Donated exclaimed. And then, as if she suddenly felt the need to measure her words, she began to speak a little slower, as if she were considering each word coming out of her mouth. "I— I am not from here. I am from the other side of the wall. I came underneath the wall just a short time ago."

Jonathan and Jonet should have had something to say upon hearing this revelation, but their shock was greater than their curiosity in that moment.

"I was sent here for you—to guide you under the wall and to the other side!" added Donatella with a new earnestness in her voice.

Jonet's enthusiasm in unlocking the wooden lid—as it turns out—was due to her assumption that there was treasure below. The two of them were really after an improvement on the limited pleasures they had known. Perhaps below the wooden lid there would be the juiciest fruit. The freshest bread. Sweeter candy. Certainly not an empty hallway.

But in a flash, it came rushing back to the two young explorers. "The voice! Tell us about the voice. He knew us!" And Donatella was more than happy they asked.

"That was the King—Avinu Malkeinu†—we just call him Avinu. He is a good king! He treats us well, and he says we are important, and, and..." she trailed off. "There is so much to tell you, but for now, we must go—he is waiting for you!"

The thought of someone important—and apparently kind, as well—awaiting them sounded intriguing. But the idea of being around someone who wasn't a child made them nervous. After all, the only people they had ever known were children like them. And what if he didn't let them return home? They couldn't just give up their life in Freeman's Forest and the constant provision of the Fields of Plenty.

---

* Donatella meaning: Gift of God
† † Avinu Malkeinu meaning: Our Father, Our King

It was as though Donatella knew what they were thinking. "It will be ok. You will have enough food to eat. You will be taken care of. And yes, you will be able to come back to this side of the wall if you choose, but trust me—you won't want to." Jonathan and Jonet thought that was a crazy statement; of course they would come back. This was home! Besides, that stone wall, and everything it represented, didn't look very inviting. It was only because Donatella seemed so king, and spoke so highly of King Avinu, that they even considered her invitation.

"So, we can come back anytime?"

"Anytime."

And with that, Jonathan and Jonet agreed to go with Donatella: down into the trap door; under the wall; through the dark corridor; and into whatever it was that awaited them on the other side.

## Reading between the lines

Jonathan and Jonet, like so many of us, are afraid to respond to the Lord's invitation. We delay and come up with excuses. We rationalize and skirt the matter. And sometimes, when we are having difficulty joining the Lord, *He decides to join us.* In our story, Donatella—representing the Holy Spirit—is dispatched to intervene in in the lives of Jonathan and Jonet. Both are living lives of equal fruitlessness; equal misery; equal drudgery. The two children, understandably, hope that God will fulfill them in expected ways, and with temporal pleasures and provisions. But what if He is actually asking us to give up something? Will we have to give up life as we know it?

## It's time to give up.

False Self can be difficult to grow out of. It is common to find ourselves "stuck" in between new epiphanies that God is revealing about us and about Himself, as we desperately want what He is inviting us into: Identity, Purpose and Calling, yet, our fear keeps us encased in the shell of our False Self. What is a person to do?

The answer is the most simple and the most difficult thing we will ever do. We must give up.

Give up faking it. Give up wallowing. Give up your burdens. Give up the stiff upper lip. Give up that which controls us. Give up trying to prove yourself. Give up the spiritual hamster-wheel of performance. Give up surviving on your own strength. Give up the walls you built to protect yourself.

What do you need to give up?

In looking at some of these items, it is easy to see why it can be so difficult! These are entrenched behaviors and mindsets, and they are all elements of our False Self.

A widely circulated analogy involves the elephant that is tied to a stake. When the elephant is a baby, she is tied to a stake in the ground. It is small, and so is she. But, she quickly learns that this stake is a reality she is unable to do anything about. As this elephant matures, however, and begins to dwarf this small stake in the ground, she remains enslaved to it because of her previous inability to escape it. As a full-grown creature now, she doesn't even try to dislodge the stake, even though she could easily pull it out of the ground.

The stake is a metaphor for our False Self. It is what binds us, entraps us and restricts us. It is what keeps us from going where we need to go. It is what reminds us, through deception, that we are powerless to move beyond it. And yet, our reality is that it is as simple as giving up: in this case, giving up the lie that we cannot break free.

## The agenda of False Self

Our False Self has an agenda, to be sure: self-protection at all costs. This tends to manifest itself in four primary ways: Self-preservation, Self-advancement, Self-gratification, and Self-justification. It is true that God invites each one of us to yield our False Self to Him, but never as an unreciprocated sacrifice. He always offers us a trade, our junk for His priceless treasure. Sometimes He makes the details of His exchange known to us, and sometimes He does not. Sometimes they do feel more like a loss than an exchange, in the moment. But, as we gain clarity on His perspective, we begin to see that what He gave us in exchange was worth far more than what we gave up.

## Self-preservation

Self-preservation often involves a great disconnect between our intellect, emotions, and will. We believe one thing to be true intellectually, but our emotions/experience tells us something else. And, despite everything we know intellectually, our fears hold greater sway in a moment of crisis.

A great example of self-preservation comes from Matthew 26. Jesus tells Simon Peter that, before the night of His arrest is over, Simon will have denied Him three times. Peter, of course, refuses to accept this, and not long after, when cornered, we see him repeatedly, and more adamantly each time, deny that he ever knew Jesus. It was the worst "best friend" moment in history.

Jesus is amazing though, in how He extends to Simon an opportunity to shed his self-preservation, once and for all. In John 21, Simon Peter has returned to fishing, his old stand-by, the identity he was entrenched in before this Messiah entered his life and invited him into something greater. On one fateful day, Simon Peter has a record catch: 153 large fish. And immediately afterward, Jesus encounters him on the beach and asks him a simple, yet profound question. *"Simon, do you love me more than these fish? Do you love me unconditionally?"* In other words, *"Is your best day producing income, stability, provision, and security, better than what I have for you?"* Simon sheepishly replies, *"Lord, you know I love you like a brother."* This happens a couple of times.

And then, this Healer of broken hearts readdresses the question. He meets Peter exactly where he is at. "Simon, do you love me like a brother? And Peter feels, for the first time, the sting of Jesus's questions. It is all he can do to offer this simple response, *"Lord, You know everything. You know that I love you like a brother!"* Honesty. Simon lays it all out there in a moment of submission; He puts on no airs. He won't back down to this challenge, like he had in prior moments. But, he also doesn't sugar coat it to try and earn favor with Jesus. He doesn't improve his answer to make himself look better by telling Jesus he loved Him unconditionally. *"You know everything. You know I love you like a brother!"*

It is in this exchange with Jesus, the Messiah, the best friend who had just been raised from the dead, that Simon finally yields himself to God, and in return, God gives Simon his calling. "Feed My sheep." These three seemingly innocuous words are the culmination of all the promises Jesus had spoken about Simon throughout the Gospels. Now, in this moment, He was releasing Simon into his destiny, and where he once spent his days pursuing fish, he would now pursue people, as a shepherd tends to his sheep. God had given Simon the choice, just as we have, between defense and destiny.

I can't tell you how many times I read this story before, blowing through the details of this chapter, oblivious to the beauty within it. It wasn't until I had been brought to a similar place, a place of yieldedness to God, that the pieces of the puzzle began to fall into place. My Identity, Purpose and Calling were all contingent on this reality: I need to yield to my Father's invitations to join Him. Calling comes from our abandonment of our agenda.

## Self-advancement

Self-advancement is really all about gaining more esteem for ourselves. We want to be respected and acknowledged. Instead, we discover that "the last shall be first."

An example of this comes from Mark 10:35-41. James and John come to Jesus with a brazen request, *"We want You to do for us whatever we ask."* Wow! The nerve! But wait, isn't that how we come to Him as well? We are no different from these two brothers. *"Grant us that we may sit, one on Your right hand and the other on Your left, in Your glory."*

Jesus replies to them, *"You have no idea what you are asking of Me! Are you able to endure the suffering that I will soon experience?"* I am paraphrasing here, but what Jesus is doing is inviting these two brothers, intent on their own self-advancement, to yield themselves up for Him. Instead of being exalted, He is asking them just how low they are prepared to go.

Jesus then alludes to the exchange. *"It is not mine to give, but it is for those for whom it has been prepared."* We want ranking and position, we want our value to be proclaimed and announced, but Jesus shows us that any position we may be rewarded with comes from complete abandonment of our agenda to His, and the Father prepares the rewards accordingly.

## Self-gratification

How do we escape the clutches of self-gratification? There is always some itch to be scratched, isn't there? Let's rule out, just for this instance, the obvious areas of sin. Let's just talk about the stuff that goes under the radar. Self-gratification can include: projecting a certain image, excessive exercise, getting the last laugh, competitiveness, attention and validation from society, perfectionism, etc. There are countless ways that we look to indulge ourselves in unhealthy behaviors.

In the case of the *rich young ruler*, he resembles a lot a Christians. In Matthew 19, he comes to Jesus with a simple question, "What shall I do to inherit eternal life?" Jesus makes a point as he challenges him to keep all the commandments, to which the man replies, "All these things I have kept from my youth!" But the thing was, this man was very wealthy, and we begin to see that his wealth was a source of gratification.

Jesus extends an invitation to him: the invitation to yield. *"You still lack one thing...sell all that you have and distribute to the poor, and you will have treasure in heaven; and come, follow Me."* God extends the same invitation to us in the areas of our life where we find excessive self-gratification outside of Him.

Jesus illustrates the exchange: what He gives us in return for that which He asks us to yield up to Him. *"Everyone who has left houses or family or lands, for My name's sake, shall receive a hundred times in return and inherit eternal life."*

## Self-justification

Christians can be so focused on keeping the rules, on sin-management, and morality, that our "success" in these efforts deludes us into thinking that we have more favor with God. I remember when, in my twenties, I refused to drink alcohol, not because I thought God disapproved of it, but because I was living by a "higher standard." It turns out that my higher standard served to breed arrogance within me, and I ended up judging other people who did have a glass of wine at dinner for not keeping to a standard that I had invented. I had become a Pharisee.

There was another Pharisee, in Luke 18. He went into the temple to pray, as did a tax collector. "God," says the Pharisee, "I thank You that I am not like other people: swindlers, unjust, adulterers, or even like this tax collector. I fast twice a week; I pay tithes of all that I get." I think I have prayed similar prayers! It is as though I thought I could fool God if I just said the right words.

Jesus then reveals the invitation to a self-justifier: "Everyone who exalts himself will be humbled..."

And immediately following this, the promised exchange: "But he who humbles himself will be exalted."

Our self-justification often appears in a form of godliness. It tends to look noble, like my abstinence from alcohol. But, like the scripture indicates, I had *"a form of godliness,"* but it was devoid of power. *"Avoid such men as these."* [*]This is a poignant reminder of an arrogance I never wish to return to.

## Yielding

In each of these examples, Jesus extends an invitation to yield. Yielding is where our Calling begins; however, it is a scary thing to consider. Why do we fear yielding to God? Perhaps it is based in our misconceptions about yielding.

"Yielding is God's way of coercing me to obey Him." "God is going to take something meaningful away from me." "I won't be able to survive without _____." "I need to clean myself up before coming to God." "I have to *not* be me; He's going to change everything about me." These really are scary things to consider!

But, as the examples also show us, yielding is an exchange! What are some exchanges God promises in the Scriptures? How about beauty for ashes, joy for mourning, praise for heaviness?[†]

Yielding is not a great mystery, either. As God invites us further into our journey into Him, He begins highlighting elements of our life that He wants us to yield so that we can grow. He is specific.

And, reality is that I don't *have* to yield, but, God will allow me to experience the natural outcome of my stubbornness. Perhaps He will allow the object or subject of my longing and attachment to turn from something desired to something disdained. And, unfortunately, the result of my refusal to yield may be rock-bottom. It doesn't have to be this way.

---

[*] 2 Timothy 3:5
[†] Isaiah 61:3

God invites us to yield in several areas: Indulgences, Small Possessions, Great Possessions, Sources of Escape, Sources of Identity, Sources of Security, and Sources of Significance. Each layer is like the proverbial onion, and as each element is peeled back and yielded to Him, we see another area that has an unhealthy place of prominence in our life.

An indulgence that God revealed in my life may sound trivial to you, but it clearly held too much prominence for me; it was my favorite soft drink. It tasted so good. I really looked forward to cracking one open at the end of a long day. I even knew the right place in the refrigerator to keep it so that it would be the perfect temperature when I needed it. God asked me to give up my favorite drink.

A small possession that God had been talking to me about was my favorite pair of sunglasses. They were really expensive, and the name on the side of the frame revealed something about my status. I was also pretty sure that I looked good in them. He kept nudging me about them, but I didn't respond. After all, I had spent so much money on them, I just had to get my money's worth out of them! And then, one day, they broke, and that's when I had to yield. Why was I so devastated over this pair of sunglasses? Why did they matter so much?

Some years later, God began lighting up an area of my life that involved a great possession: my dream car. And, I am not the only one who He has asked to relinquish this type of possession. After all, a car, for many, is a status symbol, or at a minimum, is an expression of identity. It is how many of us project an image. How can I fully embrace His identity for me if I am still dabbling in former pretenses?

Our Father also likes to show us the areas where we find Escape, Security and Significance. Do I find too much validation and significance in my career title or my reputation, instead of in Him? Do I escape into television and food, instead of into Him? Do I find too much security in my steady paycheck? He knows us so well, and He knows how we hide, escape and validate ourselves. When He invites us to yield something specific, He is inviting us to discover the original and the best source in Him.

Of course, beside pleasure and intimacy with Him, there are other benefits as well. Yielding up my favorite soft drink resulted in me being physically healthier. Yielding up my sunglasses led to healthy perspective on possessions, and He ended up giving them back to me once I had gained this new perspective. Yielding my dream car allowed me to experience the great blessing of providing for someone else. Yielding my career title opened up expanded opportunity now that I was no longer tunnel visioned on my "corporate identity." Yielding up a steady paycheck allowed me to experience the miracle of God's provision. And finally, yielding up my reputation—becoming willing to be seen as a fool for Him, increased my ministry considerably.

## So Simple, but So Hard

Just let go. It is easy enough to grasp, but implementing it is another thing entirely. Letting go invokes a hard question: "How will I make it without this security blanket?"

In Self-preservation, this defense can look many different ways: Being arrogant, fake, judgmental, un-compassionate, angry, a push-over, an avoider of conflict, a people-pleaser, empty, numb, and countless others. How does one simply "let go" of such ingrained traits? It can be scary to consider letting go of these modes that can ultimately define us. *"God/Others will see that I am unworthy, unlovable, don't have it all together, etc."* The key to our freedom is in our vulnerability and transparency. But oftentimes, Guilt and Shame are barriers to being vulnerable. For the Self-preservationist, yielding may have to begin here, meeting with the Father over our sense of Guilt and Shame, and allowing Him to bring healing here so that we can move into vulnerability.

In Self-advancement, fear is usually the motivator to try and get ourselves ahead. This fear can look like bravado and assertiveness, but underlying all of this is often a dread, a terror, that our Father, Love Himself, wants to resolve in us. The challenge we often face here is this, *"Can I let go and trust my Father to care for me, to place me where I need to be, and to define my value?"*

In Self-gratification, there are often degrees of consumption, and unless it is a clear involvement with sin, it is important to understand the scale at which we participate in this gratification, from appropriate, to indulgent, to entanglement. Let's look at eating, for example. If I eat to contentment, it is appropriate. If I eat until I am full, it is indulgent. If I eat to relax, to feel better, or to escape, I have become entangled. Is eating the problem? No, eating is a reality of life. But, it is how I do so that increasingly becomes a trap. Our Father wants to talk with us about these elements in our lives. They matter to Him; He doesn't want us to be trapped by the affairs of this life. And, to prove His point, He sent Jesus to bring about this freedom as part of His mission.

In Self-justification, we live by the letter of the Law, but miss the point of the Scriptures as a whole. We supersede our Father's intent by adding our own assumptions to it. Religious zealotry, blame, rationalizing, and soap-boxing are often indicators of this mode of False Self in our life. Jesus felt quite strongly about this, and He chides the Pharisees in Matthew 23 when He tells them, *"Woe to you, because you shut off the kingdom of heaven from people; for you do not enter in yourselves, nor do you allow those who are entering to go in...For a pretense you make long prayers...You travel around on sea and land to make one proselyte; and when he becomes one, you make him twice as much a son of hell as yourselves."* This may be the hardest agenda out of all of them to eliminate.

The person who is steeped in Self-justification is often so blind to their own entanglement that it is impossible for them to hear words of truth from the Body of Christ, and even from God Himself. I know...I was one.

## Conclusion

As a reminder, Jesus's model was to remain in a state of yieldedness to the Father. It is in this state that we, like our model, Jesus, believe that God has a design for us to be part of. When we believe, we agree, when we agree we obey, when we obey we grow in authority, when we walk in authority we experience the empowerment of the Spirit, and when the Spirit empowers, we experience supernatural results.

# Chapter five

## True Identity: A Child of the King

Donatella led the way down the cool stone steps, and Jonathan and Jonet found themselves pausing at the stone floor of the passage. Their eyes had to adjust to both the low level of light, as well as the unexpected surface. Donatella was already a few steps ahead of them, forcing them to follow after her into the darkness.

It wasn't but a few paces more when the first torch they arrived at appeared to slowly emanate to life, casting the softest, warmest glow upon the stone surface of the passage. And each subsequent torch, in turn, also awakened to light as the children passed within range. In all, they counted fifteen torches, spaced far apart from each other, before the journey under the wall was complete. Before them stood a flight of steps ascending upward.

Jonathan and Jonet paused and looked up into the foreign world that was before them. With hands up to the sky—shielding their eyes from the light—the two of them were silent as could be. Apprehension clutched at their chests.

Donatella was already halfway up the steps when she realized that the children she was sent for were not following. She momentarily paused and gently reassured them. "It's ok. Everyone feels nervous when they first arrive. Come."

Donatella took Jonathan and Jonet by the hand, one on each side, and led them up the steps. With each foot placed on the next stone tread, the air began to be filled with a fragrance they hadn't known before. But perhaps they had—it did remind them of something—but they couldn't quite put their finger on it. Regardless, Jonathan and Jonet thought it smelled quite wonderful, and in a small way, they felt reassured to continue on. As they took one last look over the shoulder at the dark tunnel they had just traversed, they expected to see a trap door perched up on its side, biding its time until it could close again. In place of a small wooden lid, however, stood a beautiful stone archway—its rounded sides coming together into a point at the top. Intricate carvings were chiseled into the smooth stone surround, and words adorned the narrowest part of the arch. "To the farthest reaches I send my ambassadors. Godspeed." And on ground, at the top of the stairs, was stamped the name of the gate's destination: "The Orphans' Forest." Jonathan and Jonet furrowed their brows when they saw the name, for everyone back home would know that wasn't the right name. I was really called Freeman's Forest. *Everybody knew that.*

The most noticeable difference between Freeman's Forest and this walled city was that it was not entirely full of children. There were some, but there were also older children that didn't quite look like children anymore—more like bigger, stronger versions of themselves. Finally, there were adults. Adults of all kinds and colors; some had red hair and others brown, some with black and some with gray. Men and women, young and old, and when their eyes met with Jonet and Jonathan's, the two of them felt kindness radiating back at them.

The fragrance grew stronger around every turn and across every doorway they passed. "Welcome, children!" called out very old women that leaned out of windows that perched over the tight cobbled alleyways. It was clear that they were noticed, but they were getting just the right amount of notice to not make them feel conspicuous.

At last they found themselves arriving at a very plain looking structure, and this is where Donatella stopped. "We are here now!" She exclaimed. Jonathan and Jonet stepped forward to the door. "Is this where the voice is? King Avinu?"

"No, first we stop here. Everyone must check in here. You must knock on the door. No one may pass without first coming to this point." The children had grown eager to meet this king. And while they still didn't know anything about him, he sounded like a very kind and sweet man. But as they considered the invitation that lie before them, Jonathan couldn't help but notice just how dirty Jonet appeared, now that they were out of the forest. And she became keenly aware of Jonathan's stench—just how long had it been since that boy had bathed? As they each looked down at their bare feet, encrusted with bits of dried, cakey mud, and their ragged, brown trousers that now looked to be several sizes too small, the two children began to feel entirely out of place. Jonathan's instinct was to run back to the gate that led to Freeman's Forest. Jonet just felt like crumpling to the floor in embarrassment. After a pause, however, she knocked on the door. It caught Jonathan completely off-guard, and he froze in fear. She knocked again. And again. She glanced quizzically at Donatella, who clearly saw that her knocking wasn't working. Jonet felt the blood rush to her cheeks, and she knocked harder. Jonathan even joined in, believing that he was stronger and could really make some noise as he rapped on the door.

He nearly jumped out of his skin when Jonet pummeled the thick wooden door with one of the cobbles she had pried up from the ground. The sound of stone on wood echoed through the plaza. And in that very moment, the iron latch gave way, and the door swung slowly open.

There before Jonathan and Jonet stood a man that—for reasons unknown—sparked a deep fear within them. And before they could even react, Donatella had once again come between them and taken them by the hand.

"Come Jonathan. Come Jonet. This is how you meet the king. You must enter in."

Quaking knees would surely have failed them had Donatella not brought them assurance. First one foot—then the other—crossed the threshold of the doorway, bringing the children directly before this man that caused such great distress.

"W-who are you?" sputtered Jonet.

"I am the judge," his voice boomed. "I am the law around here. I can see you have traveled from The Orphans' Forest…Why have you come?"

Donatella explained to the judge how the children had heard the voice that called their names, and how she had been sent to guide them in their journey.

"So, you have been called, have you?" his voice seemed to bellow.

Jonet could only nod her head in agreement. The judge's white clothes made hers look so terrible, and though she had never seen a king before, she was sure she wouldn't be allowed to based on how shabby she looked. "We want to see the king." Jonathan affirmed.

"Then I will have to check the guest list, for no one may see the king without an invitation," the gravelly voice confirmed.

The judge turned from the doorway and walked over to a massive wooden desk upon which lay the largest book they had ever seen. He slowly perused the pages of it, running his finger up one column and down another. At long last, he paused with his index finger on one name in particular.

"Jonathan. Your name is on the guest list. You may enter." And with these words, Donatella ushered Jonathan through a second door and shut it. Alone stood Jonet, trembling, and hoping with all her heart for this moment to be over. The judge returned to the book and continued to pore over its contents. After what seemed like hours, he finally reached the last page, and sighed deeply. Turning back to the very small girl, his thunderous voice softened as he broke the news to her. "Young one, your name is not on the king's guest list."

Jonet dropped to the floor and sobbed. "It can't be! I heard him…" she trailed off amidst sobs. The open last page of the book was conspicuously empty. "Would you please look again? Please?" she whispered.

Her head hung down and her chest heaved with great gasps for breath.

"Please?"

He turned back toward the book, just as she had asked. A smile grew as he sat there. For there, on the open parchment before him, began to appear the most beautiful script. You could hear it taking form, as though some invisible quill were gliding over the surface of the paper—to and fro, ebbing and flowing—until the word was fulfilled within the great book.

"Jonet." it read. "A late addition to the guest list, I see!" exclaimed the judge. "Welcome, young one!" And with these words, Donatella emerged from the room beyond, took Jonet by the hand, and ushered her forth through the doorway. As she crossed the threshold, she paused at a golden placard recessed into the keystone in the arch above her:

"Welcome, children of the king."

It was an interesting statement, but it didn't hold her attention for very long. Was it supposed to mean something to her? Was it simply a metaphor? It sounded nice, and the fact that Donatella was escorting her inside must mean that she would feel included with whoever these children of the king really were.

## Reading between the lines

Jonathan and Jonet respond to the call of the Father and the drawing of the Holy Spirit. They take the first steps beyond fear and let themselves be led by the Holy Spirit toward salvation. At this point, our story gains another element: we see in the detail of the stone gateway that the children are orphans, and the home they have known so far is where the rest of the orphans live. The children begin to understand that the world beyond the wall is actually the Kingdom of heaven, and they are being invited into a new life that is far from uppity and restricting; it is warm and bright and full of life. Both orphaned children want to meet God—the great Father who called them, but we see that they must first be brought by the Holy Spirit (Donatella) to Jesus (the Judge), the one with the authority to grant access to the Father (King Avinu). And in His great Book of Life, their names are found written. They are officially orphans no longer, but their discovery of what their adoption means has only just begun.

## The significance of being a child of the King

We speak so casually about the Father, don't we? And, for the record, *casual* isn't necessarily the problem. Perhaps the more accurate term to use is *dismissive*. Perhaps we view Him as Jesus's *boss*. We pray to the Father. And, as we grow in maturity and begin to hear the promptings of the Holy Spirit and respond to them in obedience, we get to know the priorities of this Father; He begins to transition from *the* Father to *our* Father. However, it is when we allow Him to enter our dark recesses, to reveal our inner parts to us, that it really starts to get personal. This is when He transitions from being our *Father* to being our *Abba*.

So many Christians view the Father as the strict authoritarian of the Trinity, when in reality, that role belongs to Jesus Christ.* Many of us pray exclusively to Jesus because, perhaps in His humanity, we find Him more relatable. But the truth of the matter is that the Father is that Jesus is the seat and center of all authority, while the Father's desire is all about being our *Dad*. I realize that this sounds bizarre to some, but it is exactly what the Scriptures portray.

*"See how great a love the Father has bestowed on us, that we would be called children of God..."*†

*"Because you are children, God has sent the Spirit of His Son into our hearts, crying, "Abba, Father!"*‡

Abba is an Aramaic word that was used by a son or a daughter, no matter how old or young, no matter how formal or familiar, when speaking to a father. I always called my dad, "Dad." Some people say "Pop," "Pops," "Papa," "Daddy," and so on. I feel very comfortable, at this point in my journey, calling the Father "Papa." But, not everyone had a dad. Not everyone had a good dad. Some dads were flaky. Others were absent. These experiences all have a dramatic impact on our ability to come to our heavenly Father. But make no mistake, His desire is that His children all come to know Him as their Abba, their Dad, and that they come to know themselves as His beloved children.

## A child of God: no big deal

At some point along the way, this stopped being a big deal, didn't it? "I am a child of God." Yawn. We have reduced this reality to being a *classification* rather than being our source of identity and inheritance. The term, *child of God*, is probably most used as an opposite of the term, *heathen*. In that sense, where is the significance? Where is the power? Where is the jaw-dropping awe?

*"For all who are being led by the Spirit of God, these are sons (and daughters) of God."* § Sonship and daughterhood; what an incredible privilege! Jesus reinforces this concept even further when He tells us:

*"For whoever does the will of My Father who is in heaven, he is My brother and sister and mother."*** Jesus calls us His family!

---

* Matthew 28:18, John 5:27
† 1 John 3:1
‡ Ephesians 4:6
§ Romans 8:14
** Matthew 12:50

Romans 8:29, speaking about predestination, instantly conjures for many people a theological debate and a squabble over semantics. So, for this reason, I like how the New Living Translation paraphrases an incredible concept: *"For God knew His people in advance, and He chose them to become like His Son, so that His Son would be the firstborn among many brothers and sisters."* This is too much to imagine! But wait, perhaps this is all just metaphorical...maybe we are *like* brothers and sisters to Jesus. Maybe He just *loves* us like brothers and sisters.

Our Father knows we have a hard time grasping this reality, so He offers statement after statement to reinforce this truth:

*"The Spirit Himself testifies with our spirit that we are children of God, and if children, heirs also, heirs of God, and fellow heirs with Christ..."*[*]

*"Therefore, you are no longer a slave, but a son; and if a son, then an heir..."*[†]

*"You were sealed in Him with the Holy Spirit of promise, who is given as a pledge of our inheritance."*[‡]

We are adopted as His sons and daughters, and as proof of this adoption, He has put a seal on each child. That seal, that guarantee, is His Holy Spirit. And because we are sons and daughters, we are heirs, co-inheritors along with His Firstborn Son, Jesus, our "big brother."

What is this inheritance? It is eternal life: His version of immortality. And as His kingdom continues to be expanded and revealed, both in this current era and all future ones to come, He intends for us to rule and reign with Him. There is a rich and robust role for each one of us from here forward, and He is committed to preparing us for it!

## Our Father's Discipline

And this is where we get a little bit nervous, isn't it?

*"For those whom the Lord loves, He disciplines..."*[§]

Discipline is not punishment, for the record. Discipline is proactive; it is strategic. To discipline is to instruct or correct. Disciplining involves bringing us into a state of yielding.

---

[*] Romans 8:16-17
[†] Galatians 4:7
[‡] Ephesians 1:13-14
[§] Hebrews 12:6-9

Disciplining also involves tempering. To temper steel is to impart strength or toughness by heating and cooling it. To temper clay is to moisten, mix and knead it, to work it into a proper consistency.

It is probably safe to say that no one wants to be tempered by God. It sounds painful. It sounds exhausting. Is it *really* necessary? It really, really is. Our Father is strengthening us, preparing us, and developing us for our destiny!

I had been praying for God to release me into my calling for a while. I was writing profusely, I was ministering at church, and based on my belief in bi-vocational ministry, I was working in my small business at the same time. In fact, it was a Sunday morning when my friend Kurt came up to me and shared a disturbing dream he had on my behalf. In his dream, I was surrounded by black clouds circling all around, and the message the Lord gave Him for me was simply, "Do not fear."

In April 2012, as we were coming up on renewal time for our annual workers compensation insurance policy, I decided it was time to "shop around" and find a better deal. It took longer than expected to get all the details worked out, and as we were awaiting quotes from our broker, our existing policy expired. We kept pursuing new quotes from the insurance agent, but we weren't getting anywhere. It was now a month that we were without insurance, and I was terrified that we would have an accident when we were without coverage. Little did I realize that there would be greater implications than this.

We received a phone call from our biggest client that they discovered our contractor's license was suspended. Not sure what they were referring to, I checked with the State and sure enough, our license had been suspended once they received notice that we were without workers compensation coverage. Without a valid contractor's license, our clients were not obligated to pay us, and we weren't even supposed to be performing work. Panic set in, and with no visible options, we sheepishly went back to our previous insurance provider to try to renew our old policy. We were told we could not renew, but rather, we would have to apply for a new policy, and there would be a substantial down payment of several thousand dollars required to activate it. We didn't have the money. We began contacting individual insurance companies all over the country to request quotes. Our hope for salvation was in each new quote we pursued, and in our minds, we were only a few days away from a solution. However, time kept moving on, and we continued working, even without a license and insurance. If we didn't work, we couldn't earn the money we needed to pay the new insurance premium.

And then, one of my employees hurt his back. More panic came with it. How would we deal with this? How would we get through this? How would my employee be taken care of? I prayed and prayed, and at some point, God brought an idea to mind: I could talk with my chiropractor to see what he could do! We brought our employee in to see him, and within three visits, he was back to work.

We paid for the health care out of pocket, and the employee was really happy to be back to work so quickly. God had provided for this "small" need, now we just needed Him to handle the big need!

About 30 days after our old insurance company gave us the renewal quote, we finally had enough money to pay for the deposit! Rejoicing, we called them to activate our insurance policy, but they responded that, since we had waited a month to activate our policy, the down payment had now doubled! They wanted $20,000 to reinstate us. I got the call with the bad news as I walked into the coffee shop by my house. I was stunned. I picked a seat at the big work table and took a seat across from a young woman.

As I sat there reeling, the young woman asked me, "Excuse me, but do you know Jesus?" Not really interested in conversation, I responded, "Yeah, actually, I do." She went on to tell me that she had tried about five different routes to get to her regular coffee shop, but that God kept redirecting her to this particular one. He gave her an understanding that she was supposed to talk with someone, and when I came through the door, she knew I was the one she was to speak with. Then, she asked how my morning was going. I broke down sobbing, right there in front of everyone. I was out of options, out of plans, out of strategy, and out of time. I was exhausted. I was confused. Vanessa, my new friend that day, prayed for me. I don't remember what she prayed—I was still overwhelmed with emotion. But, when she finished, she gave me a word; she told me, "Your Father sees you. He sees you." It was so simple, and perhaps a bit of a vague sounding response, but in that moment, it was everything.

Seven months had passed, and my way of coping with the anxiety was to turn out the lights and lie in bed; sleep was both an escape and a desperate attempt to replenish my soul. It was October, and I found myself, once again, on my knees, asking God to deliver us. It was the middle of the night, and He had awakened me out of sleep to talk with Him. He revealed to me that night that He was not going to rescue me, and that I could stop praying for deliverance. He showed me that this process was being used to answer my prayer to be released into my calling. He was training me, proactively disciplining me for what the future would hold. He was tempering my soul. He told me that this process was required for me to move into what He had next for me. He then showed me how He was present and active throughout the entire process. He gave me advance notice of this hardship through my friend Kurt, He inspired the strategy for my injured employee, and He sent Vanessa to encourage me.

In these difficult times, it is common to wonder whether such a trial is oppression from our enemy, or a trial from God, or simply the result of human choice. I had wallowed in the guilt and shame I felt over the terrible state the business was in, and I had tried everything I could think of to withstand the enemy's involvement in the matter. But, when my Father gave me permission to stop fighting it, I gave in and decided to embrace the hardship. There was a great sense of peace in being so resigned to how the Father was answering my prayer for growth and calling. By the end of the year, the situation was completely resolved. There was no magnificent resolution; no memorable finale, in fact, the whole matter just fizzled away slowly, and life went on.

He is a Father who invests into His children, and that investment may be difficult; it may be strenuous, and it may stretch us further than we've ever been before. But the fruit of it is deeper understanding of our Father, increased intimacy, and preparation for our calling.

For some of us, however, destiny is a far-off thing that is difficult to even imagine. We are still stuck in the present, desiring intimacy, wanting to commune with our Father, but unable to do so. Why is this so hard to do?

Part of the problem—in fact, a big part of the problem, is that the Church fails miserably at defining what intimacy *actually* means. It is like being given a goal to accomplish, with no instructions on how to do so, and no description of what it means to accomplish that goal. In this respect, we truly are the blind leading the blind. I have often heard the word intimacy used in church, but always in a lofty, non-committal way, that leaves people as unclear as ever, and worse yet, assuming that since they don't "get it," intimacy must be something God has specially with *other* people.

## Intimacy with God

Let's get to the point: what is intimacy with God? Intimacy is actually a very simple thing to define. It is an authentic, emotionally honest exchange with our Father. He has always been about this; this is His way. He pursues us and looks to initiate these moments of honest dialogue between Him and us, and in the thousands of years that the Bible represents, He hasn't changed. Here are several examples from Scripture where God looked to engage authentically with people:

**Cain**, in his anger toward his brother: "Cain, why are you angry?"[*]
**Jonah**, in his anger toward God: "Do you have good reason to be angry?"[†]
**Job**, in his self-pity: "Will the faultfinder contend with the Almighty?[‡]
**Hagar**, in her fear and sorrow: "What is the matter, Hagar? Do not fear..."[§]

———————————————

[*] Genesis 4:5-7
[†] Jonah 4
[‡] Job 40
[§] Genesis 21

**Mary**, in her mourning: "'Lord, if You had been here, my brother would not have died'...Jesus wept."[*]

**Jesus**, in his great distress: "Father, if You are willing, remove this cup from Me..."[†]

**Moses**, in his apprehension: "Please, Lord, I have never been eloquent...I am slow of speech..."[‡]

**David**, in his anxiety: "O LORD, how my adversaries have increased!"[§]

**David**, in his righteous indignation: "Why are the nations in an uproar and the peoples devising a vain thing?"[**]

**David**, in his gratitude: "You are my hiding place; You preserve me from trouble; You surround me with songs of deliverance. Selah."[††]

Who on this list refused to engage with God? It was Cain. He dialogued with God, but he never went to that place of honesty with God about what was really going on inside.

God loves this kind of conversation with us, and apparently from the examples given, He is ok with our "messy" emotions, even when we challenge Him. Jonah challenged Him, and did God respond with anger? No, He responded with more questions; He wanted to prolong the conversation! When Job cried out in his self-pity, did God condemn him? No, He instead spoke truth to Job, and reminded Job of who God is.

And then we have David. David is an interesting case because we see a man who did terrible things in his life yet is remembered as being "a man after God's own heart." How is this possible? I believe the answer lies in the pattern above. We see David, more than any other figure in the Scriptures, venting to God, crying out to God, pouring out His heart, pausing, and then awaiting the Lord's response.

That is what intimacy with God is: we pour out to Him, and He responds: plain and simple. The more we practice this, the deeper the intimacy grows. The deeper the intimacy goes, the more thoroughly we get to know the heart of our Father.

In some of the cases above, He responded with His own thoughts. In other cases, messenger angels delivered His reply. In other cases, the exchange was God bringing to memory words of Scripture to remind the person of His track record. Some responses were consoling, while others were sobering. He knows what we need to hear and how we need to hear it.

---

[*] John 11
[†] Luke 22
[‡] Exodus 4
[§] Psalm 3
[**] Psalm 2
[††] Psalm 32

In the final stage of David's life, as he looked to prepare his son Solomon for the throne, he gave him this charge, and it reveals what David discovered to be true about being a man after God's own heart:

*"As for you, my son Solomon, know the God of your father, and serve Him with a whole heart and a willing mind; for the LORD searches all hearts, and understands every intent of the thoughts. If you seek Him, He will let you find Him; but if you forsake Him, He will reject you forever."*

God searches our hearts, and already understands what's going on inside us! He knows the doubts, the anger, and the conflicts. He already knows the crises of faith. Intimacy with our Father requires that we be honest with Him about what He already knows. If we don't, we really aren't being genuine with Him, are we?

What emotion do you absolutely feel uncomfortable showing God? What emotion have you been able to take to Him more easily? Anger? Happiness? Inspiration? Sorrow? Mourning? Anxiety? Apprehension? Indignation? Something else?

Knowing the Father is all about intimacy, and that is how Christianity is supposed to be. Jesus tells us in John 17:3, *"This is eternal life, that they may know You, the only true God, and Jesus Christ, whom You have sent."*

So, according to Jesus, eternal life is all about knowing our Father. Jesus also stated, *"I have come that they may have life, and that they may have it abundantly."* [*] Knowing our Father, and having that intimacy, with all of its fruitfulness, fulfillment and vitality, is what Jesus intends for each one of us.

It is in this intimacy, this process of getting to know God's heart, that He begins revealing to us who He says we are. This is the process where we begin to discover our Identity, Purpose and Passion in Him. This is what Jesus means by the words, *"that they may have life, and have it abundantly."*

## Conclusion

Sonship and daughterhood; this is where intimacy is based, and where abundantly life is found. In light of this, it makes more sense when we are told, "Whoever does not receive the kingdom of God as a little child will by no means enter it." [†] It is in this state, as little child, His little children, that we first come to know Him. [‡]

---

[*] John 10:7-10
[†] Luke 18:16-17
[‡] 1 John 2:13

# Chapter six

## True Identity: Soldiers of God

Jonathan was waiting for Jonet on the other side of *the book room*, as they later called it. Donatella was visibly excited to usher them forward and she burst out, "I have so much to show you! But, first things first."

She led Jonathan and Jonet into the very next room—a place unlike anything their eyes had ever seen. It was inside, but it was outside. It was a small courtyard, with a stream of water flowing from the left to the right side. They couldn't see where the water came from or where it went, but it didn't matter. Moss grew upon the boulders, and lichen clung to small trees. And flowers—flowers appeared to bloom constantly. As soon as one was spent, another popped up from another bud. It was a living place.

Jonathan looked here and there, and with a puzzled look on his face, he turned and looked up to Donatella. Where was the footbridge? "To cross to the other side—to enter into the house of the king—you must first pass through the stream," she informed them. It didn't take but a moment for Jonathan to rush forward. Into the stream he plunged, and under he went. As Jonet watched him submerge into the clear flowing waters, the most disgusting flush of dirt and filth squeezed from his clothing, forming an instant cloud of murkiness in the once-refreshing water. But before Jonathan even rose to the surface, the current had swept the filth away. Jonathan emerged from the water without a stitch of the old rags left upon his body, and there Donatella was at his side, wrapping him in a fresh, white tunic.

Jonet felt much more confident to proceed now that she had seen Jonathan do it. So, she took a step forward, and into the water she went. She was prepared to pop back up to the surface after a second or so, but something seemed quite wrong. She tumbled over and over beneath the surface and became so disoriented that she could not make out which way was up. Her little lungs burned, and panic set in. She flailed about desperately, and then—everything went black.

The next moment, she was up, on her feet, out of the water—naked as Jonathan was, but oblivious to it. Donatella was now at her side, draping a white tunic over her head and shoulders as well. The wind began to rustle, and birds erupted in song. And with a smile, Donatella said, "Come, children."

For such a small, plain looking structure, the building that could only be entered through the book room was cavernous. Donatella and the two children strolled along hallways and corridors. "Strange," Jonathan thought to himself, "Donatella seems taller than I remember." They entered a room that made Jonet gasp, and she stood there transfixed. Books. Beautiful books—everywhere. And as far up as she could see, there were floors and floors of richly bound volumes. Ornately carved panels on the walls gave way to rolling ladders and spiral staircases. She had never seen anything quite as majestic as this.

"What is this place?" she wondered aloud. "These books represent all the wisdom and knowledge of the king. Each one is a small glimpse into his character, his strategy, and his priorities. If you study them, you will learn about him and his kingdom!" explained Donatella.

Still in awe, they slowly proceeded away from the spectacle.

They stopped in the doorway of another great room—this one containing an enormous banqueting table. There were countless children—older ones, and even some grown-ups, gathered around. And though they could not quite make out what they were talking about, it looked like a grand old time. But the food—the food looked glorious! The fruit practically glowed with color, and the aroma of the bread nearly lifted the children off of their feet. But Donatella continued down the hallway.

"Children, our first official stop is the armory. Come with me." Jonathan's jaw dropped when they entered the massive room. Upon the great walls hung shields and swords; spears and javelins; bows and arrows, maces and countless other weapons. Certain weapons looked very ancient, but others looked like they must have come from the future. Armor of every shape and size was mounted on display. "Children, our first stop is to equip you with armor." Jonathan was mesmerized.

Donatella went on to explain that the good King Avinu had enemies that hated him, his kingdom, and anything that looked like it belonged to him. And arrows were constantly being fired over the wall in attempts to cause harm. "Children, it is important that you wear the armor I give you. It is for your protection. The enemy knows you are important and will look for an opportunity to harm you."

Jonathan's enthusiasm quickly turned. He was just a child—why would anyone want to hurt him? This didn't sound like fun.

"Children, once you get accustomed to your armor, we will commence your self-defense training." added Donatella.

Jonathan did not like the sound of this. He had crossed under the great wall in hopes of finding something better than what he already had. He was expecting good food, at the minimum. But this? To find out that he was essentially being hunted now? And that he had to wear armor? And fight? This is not what he had agreed to. A deep stubbornness sparked within him and began to fester.

Donatella could sense the change within him. She pleaded with him to reconsider, but he would not. He was convinced that life in Freeman's Forest was easier and less dangerous, and that he hadn't yet experienced anything significant enough to make him want to stay. And so, after a whispered exchange between the two, Donatella opened a small, inconspicuous door, and gave Jonathan his freedom. He turned to Jonet, half-expecting that she would see things his way, but for some reason, she did not. She wanted to see what else Donatella had in store. And besides, she could return anytime to Freeman's Forest—just as he was about to. "See you soon!" he declared boldly, as he ducked through the door and was gone.

Jonet missed her friend. She felt the loss of something so familiar to her—the last reminder of her life in the forest. But something compelled her to stay. Over the next days—then weeks—she studied the books in the library, and her heart began to accept, then agree with the words she read. Jonet didn't want to leave the comfort and appeal of the books, so Donatella brought her blankets and pillows, and there Jonet slept, every night, right in front of the fireplace.

Donatella taught her the essentials of self-defense, in a series of lessons that were alarmingly basic, in Jonet's opinion. Jonet did not feel very confident that she knew enough to defend herself, but Donatella reassured her. "Child," she replied, "Do not worry about these things. If you find yourself in danger, and you don't know what to do, I will tell you." "Will you be with me?" inquired Jonet. "My voice will guide you."

And with that, Donatella walked the young girl toward a gilded chest that had her name engraved upon it. "Go ahead, open it." The fragrance of cedar emanated from the open chest, and from within the velvet lining, Jonet pulled out a soft, skin colored device. She held it up to her eyes and inspected it. "This is my voice that I give to you, child." Donatella plucked the device from her palm and gently inserted it into her ear. "This is how I will guide you m…" Jonet jumped. "It's talking! I can hear you in my ear!" And just to show her how well it worked, Donatella lowered her voice to a whisper so faint, that Jonet was *only* able to hear her through the device. "Go ahead, reach into the chest once more" she invited.

This time, Jonet's fingertips touched something cold, and as she traced along the surface, she could feel intricate carving. From the depths of the chest, a dagger emerged, with an ornately decorated gold hilt that extended over the base of the blade with filigree and flourishes. The handle appeared large for the overall size of the curved dagger, but Jonet was caught up in the beauty of the craftsmanship.

Donatella fastened the sheath within the belt of the tunic and stowed the dagger safely in place.

"Young one," said Donatella, "It is time for your first assignment."

## Reading between the lines

Jonathan and Jonet plunge beneath the waters of baptism with the Holy Spirit, where their old life is declared dead and their new life begins. It is more than symbolic—they are reborn. The work of the Holy Spirit prepares them both to be able to approach the King. But the Holy Spirit, in our story, leads the children of the King first through the Scriptures and community with other believers, to equip them in the Armor of God. Jonathan, however, revolts at the thought of having to do battle as a child of God, and he runs away, back to the predictability and ease of the life he used to live. As Jonet pursues knowledge in the Scriptures and grows in her knowledge, she begins to experience the comfort of the Spirit, and grows more accustomed to the voice of the Holy Spirit within her. Lastly, she receives a weapon that is designed specifically for her—matched to her spiritual gifting—and she is called into action.

## Soldiers by design

There are many Christian books out there these days that are intended to inspire Christians to discover the warrior within. I appreciate the intent behind this emphasis, but as we talk about this further, we will use a different word: *soldier*. And, as we develop this theme here, the reasoning will become increasingly clear. At the core, the words *warrior* and *soldier* can imply different things, and if we misunderstand our calling, we may inadvertently misplace our efforts.

## Warrior vs. Soldier

What comes to mind when we think of a warrior? I equate a warrior with a person who is driven by their own cause; a person fueled by emotion; a person reliant on their own resources; and a person whose perspective of the battle is limited to what they observe firsthand. The word "warrior" implies ferocity, but it also tends to denote a bit of recklessness, perhaps even a wild pursuit of danger.

Let us now contrast the warrior with the soldier. The soldier is motivated by their commander's cause; is driven by instruction; is reliant on the kingdom's resources; and is a person who has the benefit of the commander's comprehensive view of the battle.

The warrior is an exciting model to emulate, for sure. I tend to think of the warrior as the modern anti-hero: brave, unconventional, anti-establishment, and a bit of a loose cannon. This sounds like more fun than being a soldier who has to follow orders and stay in line.

The term "soldier" portrays a different kind of fighter: one that is trained, one that is armored, one that is properly equipped, one that is regimented, one who clearly understands role and rank, and finally, one who precisely follows orders.

Soldiers. The Bible uses this term repeatedly. A soldier is part of an army. An army is led by a commander. Armies have divisions: infantry, heavy infantry, cavalry, heavy cavalry, artillery, snipers, armored divisions, and countless other areas of specialty. Each serves a specific purpose to the overall battle campaign.

## Militia vs. Army

Do we see ourselves as part of such a system? I believe I speak for Christians in general when I say that we do not. We instead view ourselves as part of a militia. How is a militia different from a standing army? A militia consists of the citizens of a community who are first and foremost farmers, merchants, ranchers, artisans, and the like. In times of conflict, these people are expected to put down their shovels and pick up their weapons and report to the battle. Militias are expected to provide their own weapons, provisions and clothing.

Is this how you see yourself? Is your primary identity wrapped up in your profession? Do you live your everyday life, just hoping that peace does not give way to conflict, and that you will not need to report for duty?

The Scriptures present a different picture. We are called soldiers and we serve in a standing army. Our primary identity is not our career, but our service as a soldier. As part of a professional army, our uniform is provided. Our provisions are provided. Our weapons are provided. Our training is provided. Our compensation is provided as well. After all, *"Who at any time serves as a soldier at his own expense?"** And, there are rules of decorum. *"No soldier in active service entangles himself in the affairs of everyday life, so that he may please the one who enlisted him as soldier"* (2 Timothy 2:4).

Don't we tend to view this passage as instruction to not get involved in sin? That certainly applies, but it is really talking about how an active duty soldier stays focused on his orders. He doesn't return to civilian activity. He doesn't pursue his "farming" or "build his portfolio;" he is always, 100%, a soldier. He lives in uniform, ready at a moment's notice to obey his commanding officer's orders.

Who is our commanding officer? Our C.O. is Jesus Himself. He told Joshua, *"I indeed come now as Captain of the host of the Lord."†* He had His sword drawn! Jesus is not a bureaucrat, He is Almighty. *"The Lord is a warrior, the Lord is His*

---

* 1 Corinthians 9:7
† Joshua 5:14

*name.* "* Our role as soldiers is to receive our marching orders from Him and obey. We do not go off half-cocked and play "Rambo" on the battlefield. We do exactly what He tells us to do. We operate in the skill that He assigned to us. And, since we know the victory is His already, as His soldiers we get to participate in those victories!

Of course, every soldier wears a uniform. Ephesians 6 describes the armor of God: the belt of Truth, the breastplate of righteousness, the shoes of the preparation of the gospel of peace, the shield of faith, and the helmet of salvation. Why is it called *the armor of God*?

Isaiah 59 describes God putting on righteousness like a breastplate, and a helmet of salvation, and He put on garments of vengeance for clothing and wrapped Himself with zeal as a cloak. Why did He suit up? He put on the armor because He was about to wage war with His enemies and to repay wrath to His adversaries. He was about to reestablish the fear of the name of the Lord.

We suit up because He does! We wear the same armor that our God wears! And, just to set the record straight, the armor is not just to protect ourselves from wounding. When we suit up in His armor, we are sending everyone a message that it is "go-time!" We suit up because we are marching with Him!

## Our Allies

I think that many Christians imagine spiritual warfare consisting of a Christian "resisting" the evil one: in other words, people versus demons. If that is the whole picture, then it can certainly seem a bit lopsided. So, just as a reminder, let us take a quick look at how the Lord has set up His army.

The Father + the Son + the Holy Spirit + Seraphim + Cherubim + Archangels + 2/3 of the Angels + Children of God

versus

the adversary (Satan) + 1/3 of the angels, now called demons

We are part of an army that is unstoppable, and our enemy's numbers cannot compare to our own. We fight alongside indescribable, supernatural teammates, as Elisha's servant discovered.[†] Furthermore, we are assigned protection by angels doing the will of God.[‡]

---

[*] Exodus 15:3
[†] 2 Kings 6:16,17
[‡] Matthew 18:10, Acts 12:13-16, Hebrews 1:14

Who are we about to wage war with? *"Our struggle is not against flesh and blood, but against the rulers, against the powers, against the world forces of this darkness, against the spiritual forces of wickedness in the heavenly places."*\*

I have heard the question asked, "Why didn't God just eliminate Satan back when Satan rebelled?" I see an answer emerge in the Scriptures. It appears that, since our enemy undermined humans at the Fall, God is allowing us to defeat that same enemy, facilitated by the authority of Jesus Christ. We also know from 1 Corinthians 6:3 that demons will be judged by humans. It appears to me that God's intent in spiritual warfare is the constant frustration of the enemy's plans by plain old human beings. Satan, the one who asserted himself as God's replacement, is stymied over and over, by us. How ironic.

What about weapons? We are given the picture of a sword: the sword of the Spirit, which is the word of God. Since, at the time Ephesians 6 was written, the Bible was not complete, what did Paul mean by *the word of God?* We have further insight with his statement, *"...the sword of the Spirit, which is the word of God. With all prayer and petition pray at all times in the Spirit..."* There it is. The word of God, as Paul intended, is wielded as we pray in the Spirit. What does this mean? Praying in the Spirit is when we speak to God and God speaks to us. It is a dialogue. The sword of the Spirit is His voice, and every time He directs, and we follow, we swing that sword. It is razor sharp and precise because He knows exactly where it needs to strike. Let me sum up 2 Corinthians 10:3,4. "Even though we live in the physical realm, we don't fight a physical war. Our weapons are not tangible, but God empowers them so greatly that they can destroy fortresses."

We are, of course, talking about spiritual warfare. I used to think spiritual warfare was a specialty, meant only for select Christians that were "called" to it. These Christians had special ability or extended training to qualify them for this ugly task. And, of course, there have been so many caricatures of what happens in spiritual warfare; why in the world would anyone want to be part of it? My wife had incredible experience and training in it, so for the first decade of our marriage I deferred to her to be the "fighter" in our family. Wow! Was I wrong! I was neglecting part of my calling by avoiding this reality!

When God started making me aware of this great neglect, I was pretty terrified. But, God showed me something that, while mind-blowing, was pretty intuitive. You see, He showed me that spiritual warfare looks different for everyone. My wife's experience and gifting had uniquely prepared her for the *kind* of warfare she was called to. Amazingly, I was designed to fight differently. My gifts and experience were to facilitate a different role in spiritual warfare. And, at the very simplest level, He showed me that spiritual warfare consists of Him making me

---

\* Ephesians 6:10-13

71

aware of a battle, giving me specific instruction as to how I must proceed, and it depends on my obedience. Pretty simple.

As soldiers, our fight is not in the temporal realm, but in the spiritual realm. As such, our armor is visible to our enemy. He knows when we are suited up. We are on the battlefield with the rest of the Lord's army—our brothers and sisters, the angels of God, and of course, Jesus Himself—our Commanding Officer.

The armor of God does not only protect me or you individually, it protects us as a community: your body and His Body. The Body of Christ was designed to rely heavily on each other for protection, support, encouragement, strengthening and inclusion, just like a platoon of soldiers does in real life. This is why Hebrews 10:24-25 urges us to not forsake assembling together; fellowship is not simply about coffee and donuts, it is the vital and supernatural linking of ourselves together with our Commander.

How do we know what is going on in this realm? Well, that is where discernment comes in. Hebrews 5:14 tells us that discernment applies to all of our senses, and that we should exercise them: sight, hearing, touch, taste, smell, and intuition. Some Christians have visual discernment and can sometimes see what is happening in the unseen realm. Others can hear the lies and strategy the enemy is trying to use. Others have a sense of what is happening through their intuition, and so forth. And for those who do not consider themselves to be very sensitive at all, we need to rely on the Holy Spirit within us to *"teach us all things"** in the moment as these opportunities present themselves.

Our instructions for warfare can be summed up in James 4:7, *"Submit therefore to God. Resist the devil, and he will flee from you."* Again, it involves us listening to God and obeying as He directs our battle instructions against the enemy. Resisting, of course, is not just standing there, suited up in our armor. It involves our weapons. Resisting is not just bracing for the onslaught, it is an active offensive move against our attackers.

## Roll Call

Admittedly, our duty as a soldier is a serious matter, and most of us would rather be doing something more entertaining and pursuing our own agenda. Paul acknowledges this when he cautions us, *"No soldier in active service entangles himself in the affairs of everyday life..."* A soldier is all about his commander's assignment.

In the physical world, a soldier's assignment puts her where her commanding officer knows she needs to be, and in the spiritual realm, it is no different. Our Commander, Jesus Christ, assigns us where He knows our souls are best suited.

---

* 1 John 2:27

## Training

In the physical world, a soldier goes through basic training and learns the foundational elements of his or her role. Beyond this, a soldier attends special schools that are designed to teach a specialty. Even further are officer schools and war college, where soldiers can learn advanced warfare technique and leadership skills.

We know that the Lord invests similar training into us as well. Because we are His beloved, and because there is so much at stake in His kingdom, He teaches us discipline.[*]

## Battle

While there is certainly spiritual battle occurring at all times around us, a good soldier remains in contact with the Commander for his marching orders. A foolish soldier ignores instruction, or may even rush in to a situation he is not assigned to. The Lord sees the whole battlefield, and He assigns a soldier or group of soldiers where He chooses.

## Hospital

Soldiers need to be cared for. Some have old wounds that require deep healing. Others are simply exhausted and need to rest. Perhaps others are malnourished and need recovery. There are seasons for every soldier when the Lord knows we need healing and He takes us out of action.

These are the stations that the Lord assigns His soldiers to. However, there are two more stations where a soldier may end up, and I fear that most of us fall into these next two categories.

## Prisoner of War (P.O.W.)

In the physical world, countries use prisoner of war tactics against their captives. This includes: boredom, confinement, danger, family separation, fear, guilt, humiliation, isolation, threats, and unpredictability.[†] How many of us do these words describe?

Prisoners of war have their identity stripped away: uniform, rank, and chain of command are eliminated. They are, in turn, assimilated back into a civilian environment, sometimes among enemy civilians. They are demoralized: stripped of hope, ambition and purpose. And finally, a soldier's identity is replaced with a new one—one that is fearful and forgetful of his true power and authority.

---

[*] Hebrews 12:6-9

[†] Textbook of Military Medicine, Office of the Surgeon General, United States Army, The Prisoner of War. p. 435 1995

My friends, is this you? What powerless "replacement" identity has been constructed for you? Victim? Addict? Sports fanatic? Tough guy? Tortured artist? Conservative? Liberal? Underdog? Achiever? We all have these anemic facades that we have bought into and that have become an almost inseparable part of our False Self. These pseudo-identities ultimately prove to be unfulfillable, since they are not our True Identity.

## Absent Without Leave (A.W.O.L.)

Some Christians have fled the battle: perhaps out of fear, perhaps out of apathy, disobedience, or escapism. I think this is what Paul the Apostle was referring to when he said, *"Demas, having loved this present world, has deserted me and gone..."*[*]

I do not believe this has to be the end of the story for the soldier who has fled his post. Jesus spoke of His desire to put everything on hold in order to *"go after the one which is lost until he finds it."*[†]

## Conclusion

Our enemy employs battle strategy that is not much different from the physical world. He uses recon, psychological warfare, disinformation/propaganda, biological warfare, diversions, schemes, traps, offensive strikes, espionage, and shock and awe.[‡] And, just as one tactic becomes ineffective against us, he switches it up and adapts his tactics. We must be watchful and wary!

If we are not, if we would rather not have to bother with this spiritual warfare "exaggeration," we are easy targets to be taken prisoner. These are the same tactics our enemy uses to keep us captive—disengaged from battle and far from the action.

---

[*] 2 Timothy 4:10
[†] Luke 15:4
[‡] 1 Peter 5:8, John 8:44, Genesis 3, Acts 10:38, Acts 13:10, Ephesians 6:11, 2 Timothy 2:26, Ephesians 6:16, 2 Corinthians 11:13-14, Job 1:12

"Your first assignment, young one, begins now." And with these words, Donatella handed Jonet a small scroll, which, unfurled, revealed a message, "Make your way to the Northern gate."

"But—but, it is such a big city! How will I find it? And what do I do when I get there? Is it a difficult task?" Jonet had so many questions. But, Donatella was no longer standing beside her. All Jonet could see before her was the brilliant sunlight streaming in through an open door.

She made her way out and paused in the warmth of the light. "You've taken the first step—well done!" she could hear Donatella say in her ear. Jonet continued proceeding forward, making only slight corrections in her direction as she felt led. She didn't know where she was going exactly, but she did seem to have a general sense of the path she was to walk.

It wasn't long before she could see a gate emerging between the rows of buildings, and sure that this must be the one, Jonet's footsteps became straight and true. Upon reaching the gateway, she noticed many doors within the same arch: doors that led to countless locations beyond the walls of the city. Once again, she paused. "Donatella? Can you hear me? I don't know where to go from here."

It was at this moment that one sign in particular began to glow before her eyes. "This way to the Orphans' Forest." A forest? Jonet knew forests. She felt a familiarity in the words, and, having tugged on the straps of her armor, she stepped forward and opened the door. A tunnel lay before her, complete with torches and stonework, just like the one that brought her out of Freeman's Forest. And anticipating what the rest of the passage would be like, she hustled through it and out through the trap door on the far end.

She might as well have emerged into the Fields of Plenty, for the setting looked identical to the world she had come from. And there, as before, were children meandering between bushels and baskets of slightly wilted produce and hardened breads. There was something strangely different about these people though. Many of them had armor like Jonet was given, but none of them were wearing it. Instead, it was piled into a sack and tethered to the waist, and the children simply dragged it around behind them. "How peculiar!" she thought.

As she approached, it was impossible to ignore the fact that each of these children—with their armor dragging behind them—had gashes and punctures on their bodies. Remnants of broken arrows still stuck within the worst of the wounds. It was a terrible sight to behold, for sure. But none of the children seemed to notice the harm whatsoever. Even more bizarre was that the remaining children—who had no armor—didn't seem to have any of the injuries the other children bore. "Peculiar!" she found herself repeating.

The non-armored children looked so familiar to her—just like the friends she had grown up with in Freeman's Forest—dirty rags and all. But the remaining children—dragging their armor—wore white tunics like hers.

When they finally took notice of Jonet, she must have looked like quite the alien. What foolish girl walks around in armor? The dirty children laughed and derided her. But the children in white—their rejection hurt even more. They cast piercing glances at her and whispered among themselves. "Who does she think she is?" and, "She probably thinks she is too good for us!" came the taunts.

And then the temptation began. "Here, have some bread." One girl took her aside and began to give her the inside scoop, "This is where the best bread is found—softer than the rest of it. And if you want apples that aren't completely mushy, look over here." It was actually a relief to Jonet for someone to seem so thoughtful. And so, the two girls began to converse.

"Who are all these people?" Jonet asked her. "Well, the girl replied, glancing back over her shoulder at the dirty children. "Those are the children that have always lived here. And those," she said, motioning to the children in white, "those are the children who were on the king's guest list."

"So…all of you have your names written in the book?" "Yes." "And all of you plunged into the stream?" "Of course, silly!" she retorted. "You should know, we all got our white tunics the same way!"

"But—I don't understand. Why aren't you wearing your armor? And what about your assignment?" Jonet quizzed.

"Um, I don't know about any assignment. I just left after getting my armor," she said. "They told us we could go back home anytime, so that is what I did."

As the girl spoke, Jonet's eyes drifted to the other children in white, and back to the girl before her, when something gleamed in her periphery. She looked over to where the small glimmer had caught her eye, but there was nothing there. She returned her gaze to the young girl before her, when again, a glimmer caught her eye. Jonet instinctively reached out toward whatever it was, and though she still couldn't see anything, her fingers instantly recognized what it was. Webs. Faint, and nearly invisible, but sticky, clingy webs streamed off of the youngster's tunic. Jonet leaned in close—uncomfortably close for the young girl—and there her eyes beheld an innumerable number of strands that floated and arched, danced and contorted, all seeming to look for something to grasp.

With a quick bolt upward, Jonet ran from one armor-dragging child to another, each of whom was covered in webbing. And as each child strolled and perused the day-old delicacies there in the field, the tendrils reached out and grasped the strands that also arose from the food, almost like a powerful static electricity. With each step forward, the translucent tentacles kept transferring the child—pulling them to the next candy, the next fruit, and the next sweet bread.

Something inside her felt sick—and angry. Really angry. And in that very moment, Donatella's voice whispered in her ear. "Do you see how the invited guests have left the banquet for stale bread?" Jonet nodded in silence. "Do you notice how they have been wounded but *they* do not?" Again, she nodded. "How do you feel, child, seeing the entanglements that keep them from leaving—that trap them here?" Jonet clenched her fists. "It makes me so mad to see them this way. Don't they remember all the wonderful things we experienced in the king's house?"

"No, child, they left too soon, and in returning to the old life, they never got to see the goodness that awaited them! You must tell them, for they do not hear my voice, being so far away from the king."

"But they will make fun of me," Jonet replied honestly.

"Come, child," Donatella invited, with an urgency in her voice.

Timidly at first, Jonet climbed atop three large baskets of bread. She opened her mouth, and the words began to flow. She told of the bounty she had seen in the king's house. She quoted proverbs and maxims that he had scribed into the books of the library. She pleaded and prodded. But to no avail.

"Who made you a judge over us!" a shout retorted in response.

## Reading between the lines

Jonet is experiencing the prompting of the Holy Spirit, directing her into a small assignment. You and I experience these moments as well, when the Spirit of God nudges us, compelling us to step into the Father's agenda and trust Him to guide us as we give courageously, or pray over someone, or approach a stranger and give them a message from the Lord. The Holy Spirit guides Jonet—unsurprisingly—back into a setting she is familiar with. The Orphans' Forest. She is back in the lonely world she came from, but this time, she is there with a mission. She sees the lost, of course, but she also takes note of all the adopted children who chose to return to their old lives. They are "saved" and they have their ticket into the Kingdom, but they are living as orphans, content to eat old, stale food, when a banquet awaits them in the house of the King.

Jonet learns that, just like Jonathan, these other children have not explored the treasures and pleasures of our heavenly Father. As soon as they received salvation, they returned to their same old way of life. They all have the armor of God, but do not use it, and are suffering the wounds of a yet undiscovered enemy. And her discernment is beginning to reveal an invisible element—the webs that are entangling her brothers and sisters. The prompting of the Holy Spirit within her is fueled by a powerful passion to wake up as many Christians as possible and bring them into the bounty and fruitfulness of the Kingdom under the leadership and direction of the Holy Spirit.

And she is rejected by those she was sent to awaken.

## Children of the King are also priests.

This could be one of the least talked about subjects in Christianity. In all of my years in the church, I have never actually heard a sermon on this subject: the priesthood of believers. I've heard it casually mentioned, but this is a significant identity that applies to all Christians.

*"But you are a chosen race, a royal Priesthood, a holy nation, a people for God's own possession..."*[*]

*"He has made us to be a kingdom, priests to His God and Father..."*[†]

## You and I are priests.

We are priests, but what does that mean? What is involved with that? What does a priest do? A priest, as portrayed in the Bible, is a person chosen specially and commissioned to approach God and to minister to others. A priest was responsible for a few main things: offering sacrifices to God per His instructions, worshiping God per His instructions, and being a representative between God and man.

Under the Old Testament, the process for consecrating a priest involved three specific elements: *Cleansing* via ritual bathing, *Anointing* by the pouring of oil over his head, and a *Sin-offering* in the sacrificing of animals to God.

---

[*] 1 Peter 2:9
[†] Revelation 1:6

In the New Testament, the requirements remain the same, and to accomplish His overhaul of the old covenant and establish us as a *kingdom of priests*, Jesus fulfills all three requirements through His crucifixion and resurrection!

> **Cleansing**: *"If we confess our sins, He is faithful and righteous to forgive us our sins and to cleanse us from all unrighteousness."*[*]
>
> **Anointing**: *"Now He who establishes us with you in Christ and anointed us is God, who also sealed us and gave us the Spirit in our hearts as a pledge."*[†]
>
> **Sin-offering**: *"By this will we have been sanctified through the offering of the body of Jesus Christ once for all."*[‡]

Many of us, upon hearing this identity, *priest*, automatically default to a belief that we are not qualified for such a position. Make no mistake, we have done nothing to qualify ourselves, but if Jesus is your Lord and Savior, He is the one who has fulfilled the prerequisites for you. You are a priest, because He died on the cross and rose from the dead and revolutionized how we access the heavenly Father. There is nothing you can do about it, except to ignore it. But, as they say, ignoring our responsibility does not relieve us of it.

If we are to accept this identity as His priests, we need to understand what we are priests of. The Old Testament priests had the tabernacle first, and later the temple. Where do we, as New Testament priests, live out this role? I believe there currently are three types of temples. This isn't set in stone; it is just my observation based on what I see in Scripture and what I experience in real life. I believe the three temples are: your body, your domain, and your church community.

In order to understand these current temples, it is important to first understand the design of the Old Testament temple. The original temple had three primary areas: the outer court, where sacrifices were performed according to God's instructions; the holy place, where God was worshiped according to His instructions; and the holy of holies, where the presence of God descended and where He met the priest.

## Your Self: His Temple

Your self and mine are reflections of this same Old Testament temple. As I see it, we have three distinct components to our temple as well, and I believe that they directly correspond to the original temple. Our temple consists of: our physical body, corresponding to the outer court where sacrifices happen; our spirit, corresponding to the holy place where worship happened; and our soul (what the Bible calls our heart), where God meets with us.

------

[*] 1 John 1:9
[†] 2 Corinthians 1:22
[‡] Hebrews 10:10

Just as the priests of the original temple did, we need to "enter in" to our own temple and learn to meet God there. How do we enter in? I believe it begins with acknowledging that 1. We are an actual temple, 2. We have three distinct areas to our temple, and 3. We need to understand how they function. We must acknowledge all three of these in order to commune with God the way He intends.

Let's take a look now at these three components, and we will proceed in a specific order. First, we will look at our spirit, as it is our spirit that the Holy Spirit brings to life and is transformed into an ally of God. Our spirit is the easiest part of us to align with Him. Second, we will look at the soul/heart, and third, we will look at the body.

## Your Spirit

Our spirit was made for communion with God. And, the child of God who has experienced salvation, but has not yet found contentment in God, probably has not acknowledged his or her own spirit. If we don't recognize that we have a spirit who was made to connect deeply with God, we will not understand that it has intent, it has desire, and it has purpose. When our spirit, and its purpose, is ignored, or worse yet, suppressed, the result is that deep un-fulfillment results within us. No amount of Bible study will cure it, and disillusionment often sets in, despite our best duty to *reach* God. I like how A.W. Tozer words it:

*"The yearning to know what cannot be known, to comprehend the incomprehensible, to touch and taste the unapproachable, arises from the image of God in the nature of man. Deep calleth unto deep, and though polluted and landlocked by the mighty disaster theologians call the Fall, the spirit senses its origin and longs to return to its source."* [*]

Romans 8 tells us that, because of what Jesus accomplished on the cross for us, our spirit is brought to life: *"If Christ is in you, though the body is dead because of sin, yet the spirit is alive because of righteousness..."* It goes on to distinguish between the former and the current state of our spirit: *"For you have not received a spirit of slavery (former state) leading to fear again, but you have received a spirit of adoption (current state) as sons by which we cry out, 'Abba, Father!'"* And finally, in this state of connection, the Spirit of God corroborates, or confirms the truth that we are actually spiritually alive: *"The Spirit Himself testifies with our spirit that we are children of God..." "The one who joins himself to the Lord is one spirit with Him."* [†]

---

[*] "The Knowledge of the Holy," A.W. Tozer, p. 9
[†] 1 Corinthians 6:17

Perhaps the most well-known reference to the human spirit is found in these words, *"God is spirit, and those who worship Him must worship in spirit and truth."** 

I served as a "worship leader" for many years, and I must confess, I had no idea what these words meant. Sure, I contrived a meaning of my own explanation, but my understanding was significantly incomplete; I didn't recognize that my own spirit had a voice.

For a glimpse of what this looks like, we need to examine the context of those famous words about *spirit and truth*. In John 4, Jesus had a conversation with a woman: the setting, at a village well. Jesus asked her for a drink.

During the course of conversation, Jesus offered her water that leads to eternal life: water so satisfying that she will never be thirsty, ever again. It sounds wonderful, doesn't it? And, though this woman lacked the context that we now have, she really wanted this deep satisfying of her own thirst.

Jesus told the woman to get her husband, and in her simply reply, we have a clue as to what *spirit and truth* means. She famously replied, "I have no husband." She told Him the truth. Jesus then revealed the fullness of that truth—she had five husbands already and was living, unmarried, with a man. This is where the conversation got weird. The topic turned to worship.

*"An hour is coming, and now is, when the true worshipers will worship the Father in spirit and truth; for such people the Father seeks to be His worshipers. God is spirit, and those who worship Him must worship in spirit and truth."*

The woman understood this. She was intellectually on the right track; she was awaiting the Messiah, and she knew that when He came, He would bring the truth.

*"Jesus said to her, 'I who speak to you am He.'"*

If we aren't careful, we can miss a profound understanding here. God initiates a dialogue with a human and designs a moment where she can be honest with Him. She speaks with honesty, and when she does, He reveals more of His nature to her than she previously understood. And this all occurs within the framework of worshiping *in spirit and truth.*

It is in this conversation that we start to grasp what spirit and truth mean. Truth is the mutual truth that is exchanged between a human and her Maker. Of course, when we offer up our truth, it may not be actual truth; it will simply be the honest portrayal of our own perspective. And, strange as it may be to consider, this is exactly what our Father wants from us. He initiates moments for us to dialogue

---

* John 4:23-24

81

with Him and facilitates moments where we can be honest with Him. And as we practice this truthfulness with Him, He reveals more and more of His nature, His heart, and His character to us.

This is worship: an honest exchange.

But, this is only half of the story. Truthful exchange must occur, but it must occur between our spirit and His Spirit. Why is this? In the full conversation between Jesus and the woman at the well, He contrasts the old way of worship with the new way. The old way occurred in a particular place, in a particular building, and, since the Messiah was about to revolutionize how humanity communed with God, Jesus was foreshadowing the change that was about to unfold. God used to be worshiped in a building that housed His presence, but now, His presence was going to be housed within His people. And the way that we would communicate with His presence was a dialogue between His Spirit and ours. And in our truthful exchanges with His Spirit, He would reveal unimaginable truths about Himself and about us.

*"Eye has not seen, and ear has not heard, and have not entered into the heart of man, all that God has prepared for those who love Him...*

*...The thoughts of God no one knows except the Spirit of God. Now we have received...the Spirit who is from God, so that we may know the things freely given to us by God...those taught by the Spirit.*

*But a natural man does not accept the things of the Spirit of God...and he cannot understand them, because they are spiritually appraised."*[*]

When we worship God in spirit and truth, (1) He reveals Himself more and more to us, and He shows us who He destined us to be as well; (2) He reveals these things exclusively through His Spirit who teaches us the thoughts of God; and (3) this only happens in those who have had their spirit brought to life through salvation.

It is deeply significant that God defines for us what His nature is, because we are limited by our own intellects. His revealing is always greater than our perception. Once again, A.W. Tozer sums this us beautifully:

*"What comes into our minds when we think about God is the most important thing about us. ... Worship is pure or base as the worshiper entertains high or low thoughts of God.*

*For this reason, the gravest question before the Church is always God Himself, and the most portentous fact about any man is not what he at a given time may say or do, but what he in his deep heart conceives God to be like. We tend by a*

---

[*] 1 Corinthians 2:9-16

*secret law of the soul to move toward our mental image of God. This is true not only of the individual Christian, but of the company of Christians that composes the Church. Always the most revealing thing about the Church is her idea of God, just as her most significant message is what she says about Him or leaves unsaid, for her silence is often more eloquent than her speech. ...*"[*]

*We tend, by a secret law of the soul, to move toward our mental image of God,* regardless of whether it is accurate, or complete or not. If my perception is that God is a harsh authoritarian, that will certainly direct who I see God as, and how I approach Him. If I perceive Him primarily as allowing bad things to happen to babies, or as the "angry God" of the Old Testament, then I will certainly approach Him accordingly. This is why we must learn to give our spirit a voice, beyond that of *our mental image of God*; our intellect.

Our soul/heart (intellect, emotion & will) must be ushered into communion with God by our spirit. Our spirit *gets* it! Our spirit is an ally of God! It owes its life and vitality to Him. It is the part of us that most easily aligns with God, and as such, it is a powerful leader for the rest of our self, if we allow it to lead.

God wants this truthful exchange with us, facilitated between His Spirit and ours. This is the way we worship. But, what is worship itself? Worship is reverence, and an act of homage. Worship isn't singing, as a default, but it can be as an expression. I can worship, yet not sing; I can sing, and not worship. Because of this, it is important to not go through the motions carelessly; there is no respect in flippancy.

God has always instructed His people how He wanted to be worshiped. He told the Israelites where to worship.[†] He told them when to worship.[‡] He told them how to worship.[§] He even defined what they were to proclaim in worship.[**] That was then; before Jesus's words about worshiping *in spirit and truth.*

As God prompts you and me, in what capacity is He inviting us to worship Him? Is it in praise and magnifying His name? Is it in adoration and affection toward Him? Is it in thanksgiving and gratitude?

Also, in what manner is He inviting you to worship Him? In solitude? In meditation? In singing? In a prayer language? We must let Him define how He wants to be worshiped. And, for all the skeptics out there, this is not simply following a whim. A whim is of *our* determining. Oftentimes, when God invites us to worship Him, the timing is terrible, from a circumstantial perspective. I can't

---

[*] A.W. Tozer, *The Knowledge of the Holy*, (Harper Collins, 1978)
[†] Exodus 3:12, 24:1
[‡] Leviticus 23:37
[§] Leviticus 23:40
[**] Exodus 33:18

tell you how many times, in the midst of tragedy, He invites me to give thanks; in the midst of misery, to proclaim His goodness; and in the darkness of oppression, to praise His holy name.

Worship is on His terms.

Things change when we worship Him. We change. Our perspectives change. And often, we simply don't know what the result is going to be. I can say, however, that I have experienced firsthand the effects of worship: God makes His presence known; and we are brought into a state of yieldedness, agreement and alignment.

I remember a great worship experience some time ago, on a quick motorcycle trip from Orange County to Yuma and back. My motorcycle broke down the first day and we were stranded in the middle of nowhere. I was contemplating having to tow the motorcycle over a hundred miles back home, and I thought about how the trip would be ruined as a result. After about an hour of troubleshooting, I just asked the Father to show me where the problem was. He did, and it ended up being something quite minor. We were on the road within minutes.

I was riding the next day with my two best friends down an empty road in the California desert. There was no one around for miles; the weather was slightly overcast, and we were flanked by sharp mountains behind us and rolling dunes ahead. It was beautiful, and I, as I often do on my motorcycle, began worshiping the Lord. I praised Him for the beauty that surrounded me, I sang songs for Him, and I began to thank Him joyfully for the rescue of the previous day. I was so overwhelmed with thanksgiving that I told Him that I simply didn't have the words to express it. I sensed His invitation, in my spirit, into a very special time of deep worship together for about ten minutes or so.

When I finally told my best friends about my time of worship, one of them sat up in his chair and began inquiring as to the details: When? Where? How long? As it turns out, at the exact same time, in the exact same place, as he rode up ahead of me on that same road, the Father was inviting him into a special time of prayer; He was inviting my friend to pour out his heart and tell Him everything that was on his heart. The two of them had a ground-breaking time together, and the understanding we began to have was that the Lord was orchestrating my time of worship in order to facilitate my friend's time of *honesty* with God; that *truthful exchange* that worship is based on.

When we worship, we converse with our Abba, our Father. And, if we respond to His initiating and leading, His Spirit is released, His work is done, and major shifts occur in the supernatural realm. Spiritual battles are won, and strongholds are destroyed through worship. What else does God want to do when we worship? Again, *eye has not seen, nor ear heard*...the fruit of true worship is beyond our imagining.

# Your Soul

The soul, or heart, as the Scriptures often use both terms interchangeably, is the center of our intellect, emotions and will. It is the essence of who we are: our hopes and dreams, our fears and failures, and our experiences and expectations. It is the most personal part of our existence, and therefore, any intrusion into it can be a scary thing to consider.

How many of us have refused to talk with our Father about the secrets of our hearts, because we thought they were too shameful, or perhaps even because they were too precious to risk exposing? We all build walls around our hearts as a means of protection; for some, these walls are minimal, while for others, the walls are nearly impenetrable.

Yet, it is in this very place, our deep center, that our Father invites us to join Him. And oh, the risk that we sense when we consider His invitation! Perhaps the high priest of the Old Testament felt similar anxiety when preparing for his annual entry into the holy of holies, knowing that he was physically at risk. He still had to enter, though, for his communion with God to occur.

It is the same for us; we must enter into our heart in order to join our Father there. This is where communion occurs.

The duties of a priest are the same for ourselves as His temple, as they were for the temple building in the Bible. The priests were responsible to keep the temple pure, and so we must maintain purity in our hearts. But, the priests also needed to care for the temple building, as we also should tend to our heart. If we continue to perpetuate the myth that our hearts are irrelevant, dismissible, even confusing our heart with our flesh, then we will never be able to enter into the most sacred place of the temple of the Lord. It is this special place, His modern holy of holies, that He descends into and fills with His presence. It is here, in His holy of holies, that He speaks to His priest: you. If you do not recognize the voice of God in your own life, it may be necessary to ask the question, "Do I enter into my own heart, or do I stand guard outside of it and refuse to grant access?"

Despite our efforts to vilify our hearts, we cannot escape the fact that God made our hearts in His image. Our hearts function just like His does: His intellect[*], His

---

[*] 2 Kings 10:30

emotion*, and His will†. Our hearts think‡, feel§, will**, speak††, and imagine‡‡, among other things, just like our Father's heart! When we enter into our heart with Him, we are joining our heart with His, and that is exactly when and where we begin to understand His heart, and in the process, understand our own. In short, this is where we get to know who our Father is.

The relationship between our spirit and our soul, or heart, is an interesting one. My spirit, a devoted ally of Jesus Christ, has the capacity to illuminate the secret places of my heart, just as the holy of holies resided within the lamplight of the holy place. Proverbs 20:27 states, "The spirit of man is the lamp of the LORD, searching all the innermost parts of his being." Our spirit is looking to illuminate, looking to facilitate our communion with the Father in our heart.

It is in this context that the words of Hebrews 4:12-16 finally make sense: the word, both the written Scriptures, as well as His active speaking in our heart, "is living and active" and able to distinguish our spirit from our soul/heart with surgical precision. In doing so, our Father is able to discern the intellect and will of the heart. And because of this, the passage tells us, we can draw near to our Father, boldly, just like Jesus, the high priest whom we serve as ministerial priests. Our access to the Father has nothing to do with the contents of our heart; instead, it has everything to do with Jesus Christ bringing our spirit to life through salvation§§, and our response as priests to enter in to the holy of holies to encounter the Father there.

## Your Body

There are two opposing portraits of the body in Scripture: that of *sarx* (Greek for *flesh*) and that of *soma* (Greek for *body*). Unfortunately, one gets all the attention and the other is overlooked. When Paul makes the famous statement, "For I know that nothing good dwells in me, that is, in my flesh..."*** he is using the word *sarx*. Christians have latched onto this portrayal as if it were a permanent statement, an absolute truth. The takeaway from this Christian philosophy, then, is that my body is bad, it works against God, and since it is a temporary housing for my spirit and soul, it is good practice to put my body down verbally, and for many, physically. And, we make it seem really spiritual by saying that Paul advocates this.

---

* Genesis 6:5,6
† 1 Chronicles 17:19
‡ Genesis 6:5
§ Leviticus 26:16
** Exodus 35:5
†† Genesis 17:17
‡‡ Genesis 8:21
§§ Romans 8:10
*** Romans 7:18

Paul, however, has been misrepresented. For he goes on to say, "Your body is a temple of the Holy Spirit who is in you...you are not your own."* Is this a contradiction? How can the body be both evil and holy? The word that Paul uses here is not *sarx*, but *soma*. Why would Paul choose different words for different portrayals of the body?

I believe it comes down to perspective, and begs the question, "Which version of your body are you committed to?" *Sarx refers to 1. the body of a person, and 2. the animal, or sensuous nature of a person. Soma refers to 1. the living form of a person, and 2. a number of people closely united into a mystical family. Sarx* is hedonistic, *soma* is holy. *Sarx* is unredeemed, *soma* is redeemed. *Sarx* is the old man, *soma* is the new man.

And for this reason, Paul encourages us to put off the old man, and to put on the new man. I believe that if we are to consciously do so, we must believe that the new man exists, and that if we are able to intellectually choose this way of life, that a big part of this transition is based in changing our perspective of our body.

In other words, if we believe we are rotten, we will inherently tend toward rottenness. If we believe that we are the holy home of our Father, we will, more and more, tend to walk in agreement with this truth. I believe that our Father wants us to view ourselves as His temple, a special place that He calls home. Romans 8:30 tells us that He has gone so far as to glorify us! What does glorify (doxazo) mean? It means to praise, magnify, celebrate, honor, to adorn with lustre, to clothe with splendor, to cause the dignity and worth of some person to become manifest and acknowledged.

This only makes sense in the context of His children now being *soma*, both as individuals, and collectively as His supernatural Body. If our Father glorifies and proclaims the worth of our bodies, then, we need to acknowledge that our enemy's efforts are to do the exact opposite. Our enemy works to distort body image, to afflict people physically, and finally, to get people to harm themselves. Whether it is through the pain of cutting or the pleasure of self-medication, the outcome is physical ruin. Our Father proclaims the value of His creation, us, while our enemy looks to destroy it.

Some in the Church have even been deceived into thinking there is spiritual value in self-harm, and there have been many versions of this throughout the centuries. *Asceticism* is an extreme form of abstinence and self-denial. *Mortification* is an effort to bring about spiritual results by living in voluntary distress, self-inflicted pain or suffering. Most common, however, is *false humility*, which is having a lowly view of oneself, contrasted with true humility, which is our agreement with God's true view of our self.

---

* 1 Corinthians 6:19

The Father has always been jealous over the sanctity of His temple, and if we recall Jesus's example when He purged the temple of the vendors and moneychangers, He was angry over the disrespect of His Father's house. And since His temple is no longer a building—you and I are, it is safe to say that He is just as protective of the sanctity of our bodies as well.

Behaviors of self-loathing, over-indulgence, self-medication and false humility are ways that we can dishonor the temple of the LORD. It is no different now than it was in Scripture:

"A son honors his father...Then if I am a father, where is my honor? ...Where is My respect?' says the LORD of hosts to you, O priests who despise My name. But you say, 'How have we despised Your name?' You are presenting defiled food upon My altar. But you say, 'How have we defiled You?' In that you say, 'The table of the LORD is to be despised.'" Malachi 1:6,7

The priests in this example were going through the motions and technically doing what they were supposed to do. But, their actions were undermined by their perspective of the altar, which they had criticized. Is this what happened with Cain? Is this why his offering wasn't acceptable before God? Is this what you and I do with our bodies?

The reality of our body is that it only displays the symptoms of what is really going on in our heart. We have all heard the following scripture but agreeing with it is another matter: "But the things that proceed out of the mouth come from the heart, and those defile the man."* We must engage our heart and enter in if we are serious about doing business with God. Our body will then display the fruit of this transformation.

## How the Temple functions

As we mentioned earlier in this chapter, our spirit can usher our heart into communion with God. There are many instances in Scripture that affirm this. The cry of Jeremiah's spirit laments, "We lift up our heart and hands toward God in heaven..."†

As our spirit aligns with the heart of the Father through the Holy Spirit, it shows our heart that it is safe to proceed. As our heart begins to move into agreement with the Father, He leads us gently into the healing of our wounded, disconnected, and fractured soul: our intellect, our emotions, and our will, and our need for escape, for hiding, for adventure, and for pleasure begins to be met by Him alone. And finally, as we begin to experience such healing, our bodies follow suit.

---

* Matthew 15:18
† Lamentations 3:41

Cravings tend to dissipate, we begin to be more comfortable in our own skin, and our physical health increases as we no longer need the self-medications we once relied on.

## Conclusion

I like the Apostle Paul's perspective on being the temple of God.[*] He takes the position that he has a lot of freedom to participate in everyday life, but acknowledges that there are elements that just aren't healthy for him to take part in. He refuses to be mastered either by physical need or by indulgence. And just as the stomach was made for food, and food for the stomach, our body is for the Lord, and the Lord is for our body!

"God wants the whole person and He will not rest till He gets us in entirety. No part of the man will do."[†]

---

[*] 1 Corinthians 6:12-13
[†] A.W. Tozer, The Pursuit of God p. 101

# Chapter eight

## True Identity: Prince and Princess

A hard biscuit came flying out of nowhere and struck Jonet smack dab on the lips, just as she was reaching the most impassioned part of her plea to the children. "Stop trying to change us! We like it here!" came a yell from the same source as the biscuit. She was stunned. She didn't so much feel *pain* as she did *shock*. And when she turned her head to see where it had come from, her heart sank. For there, trying now to look inconspicuous, was Jonathan. *He* had thrown the bread at her. *He* had humiliated her. It was too much for a young girl to bear, and she burst into tears, running all the way back to the trap door. She bolted through the tunnel and back into the city, where she collapsed to the steps and wept.

Donatella was right there, and as Jonet sobbed and sobbed over the betrayal and humiliation, Donatella held her and listened to her pain.

"I am so sorry, my child. But you must know that when they insult you and cause you pain, it is only because of what you represent. Come, I know what you need right now." And with these words, Donatella took Jonet by the hand and led her back to the house of the king.

Beyond the banqueting room, the library and the armory, they walked hand-in-hand until there was no more hallway left. Before them stood an open doorway that held no door. "After you, child," Donatella's voice reassured. Jonet entered the room and quickly scanned to see if there was something obvious she should take note of. It looked like a big comfy room. A large, overstuffed and tufted sofa sprawled in front of a crackling fire. A colorful and intricate coat-of-arms hung above the mantle. And off to the side was a single chair on a raised platform, with a wooden desk to its side.

Two distinct voices became apparent to Jonet, as if they were not yet in the room, but were soon approaching. And just as they both became clear and she could make out some of the words, two men walked into the scene before her. One was the judge, who noticed her and beckoned. But the other man she did not recognize.

"Avinu, this is the child I was telling you about!" exclaimed the judge. "Ah, yes, Jonet. She has such wonderful strength—always has," expressed the other proudly.

And suddenly it hit her—this, this was the king! "King Avinu, your excel—I mean, your majes…" The king chuckled, and with a grin that warmed her heart, he said, "My name, child, is Avinu Malkeinu. Those who fear me call me *the Great King*. Those who are indifferent don't believe that I even exist; but those whose names are on the guest list—well, they just call me Avinu. That, my child, is what you may call me. And now, just look at you. You are getting so big!"

"Jonet, would you like to see something special?" asked the judge. Well, certainly, in a place like this, and in front of the king, why in the world would anyone say no? She nodded quickly.

The judge and the king and Donatella all strode through the doorway and into the hall, and after only a few quick turns, they paused in front of what was clearly a bedroom. The fragrance of moss and pine gently emanated from somewhere in the room, and it reminded her of the forest she grew up in. On a nightstand she spotted a stand that was the perfect shape to hold a curved dagger. And the bed— it was so tall and billowy—she thought it might make a wonderful room for someone.

"Child," said the judge, "In my father's household there are many rooms. I prepared this one just for you."

"Really?" blurted Jonet. "But, I don't understand. Why me? I don't deserve this."

"My child," said the king in the gentlest of voices. "Did you not see the sign after you were granted entry into my home? It said, 'Welcome, children of the king.' Did you not believe its words?" Jonet shook her head no, and puzzled, she asked, "I grew up in Freeman's Forest. How could I be your child? I've only just met you! It sounds wonderful, but I just don't understand."

"Oh, dear one—that is not the true name of the forest. That is what my enemy calls it in order to deceive the inhabitants into believing that they are free and uninhibited. No, the true name is the *Orphans' Forest*, for that is where all the lost and lonely—the fatherless—are abandoned. And child, you must know that my deepest desire is to adopt those lost children. That is why I called you! My son here," he said as he placed his hand on the judge's shoulder, "My son had just finished adding on your room to my house, and it was finally time to call you to your forever home!"

"You can explore every corner of my—of *our*—father's house. Everything here is yours," promised the judge. And with a smile, he added, "You know, this makes us brother and sister now! Why don't you call me Brother Prototokos[*]—or just *Proto*, if that is easier."

"There's one more thing, little sister," said Proto as he pulled open the top drawer of Jonet's new nightstand. "Since you are a daughter of the king, I give you a token of your adoption into this family." And with these words, Proto took in his hands a golden brooch and pinned it upon Jonet's white tunic, directly above her heart. It was rather large, about the size of the palm of her hand, and it appeared somewhat like a cross between a coat-of-arms and a crown. The upper portion was a crown—not a simple circle with points, but rather, one of those elaborate crowns where gold straps rise vertically from the base and meet in the middle at the top with a small cross at the tip. And at the base was an unfurled scroll with the king's family name on it, "Malkeinu."

"This crest I give you," cautioned Proto, "is more important than the armor you were given by Donatella. Do not lose it. Do not give it away. While your white tunic communicates that you have been adopted by the king, this crest states that you have been given royal authority to act on his behalf, at his direction."

Jonet was trying to take it all in, and if she were honest, she would have to admit that she didn't really understand the significance of what Proto was saying. But her hand instinctively rose to her heart and she softly placed her hand over the brooch, as if to both acknowledge it and keep it safe, all in one motion.

"Avinu?" she asked. "Donatella told us that we could go back to the forest anytime. But can we also come back here anytime?" King Avinu could see the concern in her eyes. "Are you worried about Jonathan? he inquired. She simply nodded. "I love being here, but I really miss my friend."

"My child," Avinu began—and each time he called her such, her heart warmed more and more. "My child, coming and going doesn't happen more than once or twice. When an orphan experiences everything that the kingdom has to offer, and he still chooses to return back to an orphan's way of life, there is very little chance that he will ever want to come back. Now, in Jonathan's case, he doesn't know what it means to be part of the kingdom. He grew fearful in the armory and left, and has never experienced anything further. There is still opportunity to win him over. But it will require that you appeal to him as an ambassador of the king. Are you up for the task?" he asked. And without hesitation, she exclaimed, "I am!" But she caught herself. "The last time I saw him, he hurt me! He acted like a completely different person! What if he treats me like that this time as well?"

"My child, remember that he is still the same orphan at heart as he was before you both first came here. *You* are the one who is changing. The Fields of Entanglement

---

[*] Prototokos meaning: Firstborn over all Creation (Col. 1:15)

have a strong grasp on his need for security and provision, and you will have to convince him that something greater awaits."

As soon as these words were spoken, Donatella came around the corner and into Jonet's room.

"It is time, young one. Come with me," she invited.

## Reading between the lines

Jonet steps out courageously and follows the prompting of the Holy Spirit, and in the process, she is rejected by the very Christians she is trying to awaken. She retreats into the safety of the Holy Spirit's comfort, and she is led straightaway to the presence of her heavenly Father. As she meets Him, she discovers an affection and approval from Him that supersedes any validation she had ever imagined possible.

As she is shown the room that was prepared for her, she experiences a sense of belonging within her Father's house. And finally, Jesus gives her a badge to wear upon her heart. This badge is a symbol of the royal authority of Jesus Christ—the very authority He has given to us and expects us to walk in. It is a sign to the spiritual realm that we belong to the King of kings, and it is a reminder to us that we are now a part of the royal household.

## A Royal Birthright

It is pretty straight-forward, and yet, we minimize and under-estimate its significance. To be a son or a daughter of the King is to be a prince or a princess. And yes, Jesus Christ—the firstborn—our "big brother," is the one the throne belongs to.[*] He is the Crown Prince, we are not. But, we are princes and princesses nonetheless. And who is this King we speak of? He is none other than the LORD of Hosts.[†]

For most of us, this may be too hard to believe at first glance. And, with the caution of a good student of Scripture, I encourage you to examine the evidence for yourself. This is not a shady, "feel-good" idea, based on a single scripture taken out context. The portrait of sonship and daughterhood, of our adoption by the King, and of His kind affection toward us, is a theme that is woven all throughout the New Testament. It is a theme that I, quite honestly, am surprised isn't taught on more often; perhaps it is viewed as too indulgent and too self-focused.

---

[*] Matthew 19:28, Luke 1:32, Hebrews 1:8, Revelation 3:21, Philippians 2:10-11
[†] Psalm 24:10

As princes and princesses among many brothers and sisters, we are part of a very special household. *"You are no longer strangers and aliens...but you are of God's household."** We are His royal court! So, our adoption by the King was not just a transaction, a title transfer from our old owner to our new one; our adoption was a rescue from bondage, a thorough cleansing, and a place being set before us at His great dinner table.

*"But God, being rich in mercy, because of His great love with which He loved us...raised us up with Him, and seated us with Him in the heavenly places in Christ Jesus."*[†]

And, together with all of our brothers and sisters seated together with Him, we make up the royal family: *"But you are a chosen race, a royal priesthood..."*[‡]

And, being part of His household, we have full access to our Papa, the King. The fact that we are His loved ones gives us perspective on how He feels toward us. Our Father, the King, is Grace embodied, and He lavishes it on us.[§] He looks forward to us joining Him, returning ourselves to His presence as often as we can. *"Therefore, let us draw near with confidence to the throne of grace."*[**]

And though the Firstborn, Jesus Christ, will take His place as the King of Kings, we will also reign with Him.[††] We are co-heirs, not only of an inheritance, but of a vibrant, adventurous future together!

A prince and princess bear the royal insignia of the family they represent. And when we read that our Father *"sealed us and gave us the Spirit in our hearts as a pledge,"*[‡‡] it is easy to connect the dots. A seal was used to protect, to identify, and to authenticate the validity of something. Think of the seal in a king's signet ring that he would use to stamp his approval onto a letter or a decree. The Holy Spirit is what our Father stamped on us, he is, in essence, a living coat of arms. When we approach our Father's throne, that seal is visible. When we interact with our brothers and sisters, the seal upon us validates a connection with the seal on someone else; it is because of the seal that we have a connection in the first place. And, when we ride out into battle, in the spiritual sense, the seal of the Holy Spirit upon us is like the King's coat of arms held high in the air. It commands respect and submission to the King when wielded by His sons and daughters.

---

* Ephesians 2:19
† Ephesians 2:4-6
‡ 1 Peter 2:9
§ Ephesians 1:6
** Hebrews 4:16
†† 2 Timothy 2:12, Revelation 20:6
‡‡ 1 Corinthians 1:22

*"You have given a banner to those who fear You, that it may be displayed because of the truth."*[*]

We bear the King's banner, His seal of authenticity, and for good reason. We need it to fulfill the expectations that come with being a prince and princess.

## Ambassadors for our Father

First, we are to model our Father. *"Therefore, be imitators of God, as beloved children..."*[†] Everywhere we go, we are royalty. Everywhere we go, we are recognizable by the seal we bear. There is no such thing as anonymity in the spiritual realm. We can choose to not take this role seriously, but we are the only one who doesn't. Our enemy sees who we are, and he wants to make a mockery of us and the royal family, however possible.

We are our Father's representatives out among the kingdoms of this world: kingdoms that belong to the enemy of our souls. We are on foreign soil! And as a reminder, our Father, the King, has sent us a sober reminder: *"Beloved, I urge you as aliens and strangers to abstain from fleshly lusts which wage war against the soul."*[‡]

How then, are we to represent our Father in His stead? We are expected to reflect His priorities and carry forth His perspectives. And since our Father is so occupied with restoring mankind back into communion with Himself, He has made us His official ambassadors for this very purpose.

*"All things are from God, who reconciled us to Himself through Christ and gave us the ministry of reconciliation...Therefore, we are ambassadors..."*[§]

## Walking circumspectly

Second, a son or daughter of any king needs to take precautions that other people don't require. We are prime targets for the King's enemy, and he will take advantage of any carelessness on our part to infiltrate or to attack us.

---

[*] Psalm 60:4
[†] Ephesians 5:1
[‡] 1 Peter 2:11
[§] 2 Corinthians 5:18-20

For this reason, we need to wear body armor. *"Be strong in the Lord and in the strength of His might. Put on the full armor of God, so that you will be able to stand firm against the schemes of the devil."*\*

We need to take the threat seriously and recognize the fact that we are important enough in the spiritual realm to warrant being targeted by our adversary. *"See then that you walk circumspectly, not as fools, but as wise, redeeming the time, because the days are evil."*† Circumspect means to look around vigilantly. In driving terms, it means, *"Keep checking your mirrors."* In military terms, it is, *"Check your six (o'clock)."* It is not paranoia, it is being alert and aware.

## Being groomed to reign

Finally, a prince, and I will include princesses here, is expected to go to war. This has been the way of earthly kings, and it is certainly the way of *the* King. *"No soldier in active service entangles himself in the affairs of everyday life, so that he may please the one who enlisted him as a soldier."*‡

Why is this necessary? Part of the reason is that we are enlisted to fight His campaigns out into enemy territory and to claim new ground for Him. We are also enlisted because it is in battle that we learn valuable leadership lessons, lessons that we will need to draw on as He entrusts us with more authority and responsibility. And, perhaps a third reason is that, with experience, we earn the respect of those we fight alongside with, and the confidence of those under our care.

There are, tragically, those who would rather not have to acknowledge this identity. For some, the idea of being considered royalty is a put-off; in their own perspective, they associate royalty too closely with tyranny and aristocracy, and they want nothing to do with it. For others, the thought of all the responsibility is just too much to take on. They are, in essence, abdicating their royal identity.

Abdication. Voluntary surrender of your royal birthright. It reminds me of Demas in 2 Timothy 4:10: *"Demas, having loved this present world, has deserted me and gone to Thessalonica."* What was going on in Demas's mind? Was the weight of responsibility too much to bear? Did he miss the "good old days?" In any case, he fled, it appears, mentally, spiritually and physically.

In the context of an earthly kingdom, there was Edward Windsor. Edward was the crown prince of England, and when his father, King George V died in 1936, the throne passed to him. He was a conflicted man, as he had an empire on the one hand, and a scandalous relationship on the other. As it turned out, he could not

---

\* Ephesians 6:10-11
† Ephesians 5:15-16
‡ 2 Timothy 2:4

have both. And so, before he could be officially crowned King Edward VIII, he abdicated the throne. He would not live out his destiny as King or be memorialized as Edward VIII. Instead, he finished out his years holding a number of powerless, forgettable roles that had nothing to do with his destiny. He will be remembered as the English monarch with the shortest reign in history.

I realize that at some point, this earthly metaphor falls apart. But, for me, it serves as a potent reminder of a greater kingdom, of my sonship, and the authority and destiny that God has promised to me as His child. *"Greater works than these he will do..."** What about you?

For all the parents that read this book, consider the implications for your children. We can look at our children and see in them potential sons and daughters of the King too! Our children can be the best kind of prince and princess imaginable, belonging to an unending kingdom. Our role then, as parents, is to raise up the next generation of royalty, to lead them personally to the King, to teach them everything they need to know about this great kingdom, and to model for them what it looks like to live as His beloved sons and daughters.

## Conclusion

Sonship and daughterhood is a wonderful, life-changing truth to become more and more acquainted with. But, as we examined in this chapter, the implications of being a son and daughter of the King are incredible epiphanies in and of themselves.

How would your life change if you began to view every moment, every exchange, and every encounter through this lens: Ambassador, Heir, Royalty? How would our ministry be transformed if we began to view others primarily this way? How would our perspective change if we carried ourselves as a son or daughter of the King? How would our behaviors change?

It's ok to consider this. It is not self-indulgent; it is right. It is who your heavenly Father says you are as His child.

---

* John 14:12

# Chapter nine

## True Identity: Spiritual Roles

Jonathan made his way down the well-worn paths that led from the Orphans' Forest and into the Fields of Entanglement. Even though he had grown tired of the provisions, and despite the deep hunger and discontent that had grown within his young body, he found himself traipsing toward the baskets and bushels as though he were craving the bounty.

He stared down at the piles of bread. He cast an apathetic glance over a mound of slightly puckered oranges. He felt compelled to return here; to browse; to eat—though he never felt satisfied.

The timing couldn't have been better. When Jonet emerged from the trap door, it was as though she knew exactly where he would be. She was running as fast as she possibly could.

Jonathan snapped out of his stupor the moment her hand grasped his. Her fingers wrapped around his small hand, and in a flash, she could feel the emptiness of his young heart. "Jonathan!" she spurted—somewhat quietly so as to not alert the others, but loud enough to grab his attention— "Please! Come with me!"

He looked at her with an empty gaze. "Jonathan, I know what you must be feeling! I can feel it too. All this *plenty* really isn't what it pretends to be. I know you can feel the emptiness it brings—emptiness instead of fullness. You and I experienced the beginnings of something wonderful on the other side of the wall—come back with me!"

Jonathan's heart to stir. Emptiness? She would certainly know, for they were both raised on the same provisions. Did they really experience something wonderful? He couldn't quite remember.

"Jonathan, look down at your clothes! You are dressed in white—remember? Your name was on the king's guest list? We crossed through the water and were washed clean? Donatella brought us into the king's house and gave us armor? Remember?"

99

And suddenly, he did. But just as the waves of memory rushed back, Jonathan was overwhelmed by the shame of having returned to the old life after being invited into the king's house. He was silent, and didn't know what to say.

"Jonathan, I can sense that you feel ashamed, but Donatella said you can come back, remember? Don't let your shame be more powerful than your desire to be back in his house. There is so much you haven't seen yet. Aren't you tired of this crummy old food out here? Come with me, Jonathan!"

She had convinced him, and Jonathan came to life. The two of them ran, hand in hand, back toward the trap door. But as they did, it was as if the field knew what they were up to, and out came the tendrils. This time, however, they were not transparent. They were obvious, and seemed to grow instantly out of anything they happened to run past. The bread sent out brown tentacles; the oranges, well, orange tentacles; and the grass, green ones. The faster the two of them ran, the more aggressive the tendrils became until they swarmed and lunged for Jonathan's foot. He paused just long enough to try to shake off the grasp of the tendrils, but in that moment, they burst forward and wrapped around his foot.

"Jonet!" he cried. "Help me! I am tangled up!" They were so close to the trap door, and to the freedom beyond. Jonet spun around and lunged for her friend with both hands now. She pulled and pulled, but could not free him from the entanglement. The struggle only seemed to strengthen the tendrils, and they continued creeping up Jonathan's leg. "This isn't working!" she shrieked in desperation.

And just when all hope felt lost, Donatella's voice sounded in Jonet's ear. "Pull out your knife, Jonet!" She fumbled around for a moment, having never used it before, but finally it emerged from its sheath. Jonet lunged forward with the curved dagger, and like a sickle harvesting wheat, she pulled the hooked tip across the strangling tentacles, and Jonathan was instantly freed. He jumped into the trap door opening, and Jonet followed behind him, dagger still out, just in case the tendrils attacked once more.

With a wary eye, she closed the trap door slowly—dagger extended out—until it was completely shut and there was no chance of the tendrils following them. Jonet slumped down to the floor—what had just happened? Did she really just rescue her friend? Were those tendrils as evil as she had imagined? She felt at once empowered and exhausted, and she sat on the cool stone floor to catch her breath.

Jonathan sat beside her, but didn't say a word. He was also trying to process what had happened. He was embarrassed that Jonet had to come rescue him. But he was also incredibly proud of how brave she was—especially after he had treated her so terribly. And thinking of how she set him free with her knife, he grew excited.

"You were amazing out there!" he exclaimed. "How did you do that?"

Between deep breaths, Jonet explained how she had simply listened to Donatella's voice, and how, if she hadn't, she wouldn't have known what to do.

And with this, she began to tell her best friend about all that she had experienced in his absence. Her own room? A weapon? A communicator? Jonathan began to feel a sense of excitement that he hadn't felt originally in the king's house. It was as though he *had* to come back to his old life to realize just how empty it really was.

The two friends sat in the cool of the passage for hours, sharing memories and laughing, and imagining what the future might look like. When they had finally caught their breath, and the shock of it all had worn off, the two stood to their feet, and began their procession out from under the wall, and into the light of the king's city.

King Avinu could not have been prouder of his daughter. "Well done, Jonet! You were so brave, and you jumped into action even though you didn't know how it would turn out—you simply listened to Donatella's directions and obeyed. I am so pleased with you!"

"And you, young man," he said as he turned to Jonathan, "I am proud of you too, for it is no small thing to escape the entanglements of the old way of life. I have so much to show you, if you will stay here in my kingdom."

King Avinu, Proto, and Donatella walked Jonathan to the room that had been awaiting him. And just as with Jonet, over the next few weeks and months, he received his crest, his communicator, and his weapon.

Jonathan and Jonet were together again, no longer just friends, but brother and sister in this fantastical new world. They grew in wisdom and knowledge, and in favor with the king and all his subjects. And for the first time in their young lives, they were content. But as they continued to strengthen and to learn, the two siblings noticed a swelling of emotion toward the life they had left behind. What was new feeling all about?

Jonathan and Jonet sat with Avinu one day in his lush courtyard where they had first plunged beneath the waters, and explained to him how they felt deep inside. "Avinu, we love it here, and we do not want to leave," stated Jonathan, "but we are feeling like we are supposed to go back to the Fields of Entanglement and the Orphans' Forest. We honestly don't know why this desire has awakened in us!"

"Ah, my children, I believe I can help you understand what is happening. What you are experiencing is normal for my children who are maturing. You have a longing toward the old world and the people within it, because your deepest desire

101

is to rescue them and bring them here. You are feeling what I feel, because, as you get to know me, you become more and more like me. Jonathan and Jonet, this longing is welling up within you at this moment in time, because your next assignment is coming due. Enjoy your time in the garden today, and tomorrow we will get started."

"Jonet," Avinu added, "you have already had a taste of the role I have reserved for you in my kingdom. Every assignment I send you on is for the purpose of spreading my kingdom, and you, Jonet, have the role of rescuing people that are stuck in the clutches of entanglement. I have given you a small dagger, because as you have already seen, you get up close and right in the danger with the person you are rescuing. You have a small weapon for tight quarters."

"Jonathan, however, you have a different role to play. What do you think the purpose of your weapon is?" Jonathan thought to himself for a moment, they replied with as much confidence as he could muster. "Avinu, you gave me a javelin, so my role is to target the dangers that are further away—I think." Avinu chuckled, "That's right, Jonathan, precisely. Your role will be to strike the enemy in very pin-pointed ways. And just like your sister experienced, Donatella will guide you when the time comes."

## Reading between the lines

Jonathan has spent enough time back in the old life to become entangled in the affairs of the world, but also to experience the deep discontent that comes with it. And, as is often the case, the Lord uses our brothers and sisters in Christ to speak truth to us and lead us to freedom. In our story, Jonet is fulfilling that very role, led by the Holy Spirit. Both of them, ultimately, begin to feel a growing passion to reach out and bring freedom to Christians who have become entangled in the affairs of the world, and who have yet to experience any real connection with their heavenly Father. Our passion is an indicator of the role that God designed us to fulfill.

## You have a one-of-a-kind purpose.

There is a widely accepted saying in the church today which goes something like this: "There is a God-shaped vacuum in the heart of every man which cannot be filled by any created thing but only by God, the Creator, made known through Jesus." This saying has been attributed to Blaise Pascal, C.S. Lewis, and St. Augustine. However, no one seems to be able to verify that any of them actually said this. This quote actually appears to be a distortion of something that Blaise Pascal wrote in his masterpiece, "Pensees."

Concepts such as this can be misleading if taken only at face value. You see, we expect that once we are "saved," and therefore are now "filled" by God, that there is nothing left to desire. And based on this belief, we launch into our Christian life

102

with all the expectation that we should be living fulfilled, joyful, enriched, empowered, and authoritatively, all because God has "filled" that hole in our hearts.

This expectation is further bolstered by the illustration of the cross bridging the gap between one cliff and another. The cliff on the left is said to represent mankind, and the cliff on the right is said to represent God. The cross that bridges that chasm clearly represents the atoning work that Jesus did on the cross.

Both of these examples are viable representations of what truly happens at the point of salvation. Both of these examples are accurate as they describe our need to encounter our Creator and the method by which we must do so. However, what both of these examples fail to illustrate is what it looks like to *live and grow* as a Christian.

I was a Christian for 20 years when I finally came to the place in my walk with the Lord where I had to be honest with myself and with Him and admit that I was deeply unfulfilled. I was miserable. I felt dead inside. And no amount of praying or reading my Bible could alleviate these feelings. Unfortunately, there are many, many Christians in this same state of existence who are afraid to talk to anyone about this reality. After all, how do you tell somebody that, although you have the Creator of the universe living within you, "It's just not enough." How arrogant! or so we think.

In reality, the vacuum model is far too limiting for God's design. The vacuum model assumes a rather static engagement with God, and in reality, serves to promote the idea of the "ticket" to heaven. In other words, once you have God, you're done. You just need to keep showing up. And one day, after enough showing up, you will die and go to heaven.

What do the Scriptures actually teach? They teach us that a profession of faith and an indwelling by the Holy Spirit are just the beginning of our growth and development as children of God. Part of this process of maturing is the necessary building of a strong foundation in our faith. This involves studying the word, memorizing Scripture, learning about how God operates in the world today, and being discipled by those who are more mature than we, and so on.

The trouble is that many Christians still do not understand that there is life beyond this. Many still do not understand that they will need to "launch" from this foundation when God begins to draw them into the next stage of maturity. Hebrews 6 speaks of this reality.

## There is life beyond salvation

1 John 2:13 describes how we begin as spiritual children, then develop into adolescents in the faith, and finally mature into spiritual adults. We transition from

becoming rooted and established to actually implementing the knowledge we have gained, and finally walking in communion with the Father, wielding the power and authority that come with that level of maturity.

One thing that is missing from the vacuum model is God's intentional design. Meister Eckart once said, *"God expects but one thing of you, and that is that you should come out of yourself in so far as you are a created being made and let God be God in you."* I would say that we often forget that God made us for a special purpose, and that he wants to infill and empower us for that purpose. But, unfortunately, the more accurate statement is that most Christians do not know this. I think most people in the church are oblivious to the fact that they were intentionally designed for something amazing. They were destined for a *special* purpose in God's kingdom. They were pre-gifted and pre-ordained for the cause that God has created them for.

What evidence is there in the Scriptures of this? And, why would we even need to ask this question? Many Christians become quite wary anytime the word "special" is applied to a person. Why is this? It is simply because we believe it is selfish and egocentric to spend any time on introspection or understanding of our personhood. It would seem that anything that is focused on "me" is selfish because it takes my eyes off of God. The reality is that God himself calls us to this level of introspection. Ephesians 4 tells us to continue putting off the *"old man."* It says to *"lay aside the old self which is being corrupted in agreement with the lusts of deceit, and put on the new self in agreement with God's design in righteousness and holiness of the truth."* How are we to do these things without examining ourselves? How are we to do this without introspection?

Augustine reportedly once said, *"I desire to know God and the soul."* *"Nothing more?"* *"Nothing whatever."* The reality is that as we grow to know God the Father more intimately, He reveals to us truths about who *we* are internally. The two are intertwined. Leonard Ravenhill often said, *"The more spiritual a man gets, the more natural he becomes."* Introspection yields understanding about our wiring, our triggers, our passions, and our motivations. So, it is not only our weaknesses that are revealed, but it is also God's design upon us that is revealed.

## The Five Spiritual Roles

In Ephesians chapter 4, God identifies five spiritual roles that He has instituted for the operation of His church. We are first reminded that we have each received of the grace of God, and then the roles are revealed: apostle, prophet, evangelist, pastor, and teacher. I believe that each one of us was designed to fulfill one of these roles. Not everyone would agree with me, however, as some Christians believe that some of these roles have "expired," while others believe they only apply to select people. I invite you to examine Ephesians 4, both as it relates to the theme of Ephesians and to the New Testament as a whole, and to decide for yourself what view you will adopt.

What do we know about these five roles from Scripture? We know that He established these roles for the equipping of the saints for the work of service, and for the purpose of building up the body of Christ. Here are their descriptions:

## Apostle

An apostle has a passion for the advancement of God's kingdom. Apostles, in the New Testament, typically perform signs and wonders. There were mass conversions as a result of people seeing the power of God through these people. 2 Corinthians 12:12 testifies to this. What was the purpose of an apostle? Romans 1 tells us that it was to bring about the obedience of faith among all the Gentiles for His name's sake. How did an apostle operate? He or she simply lived out what Jesus described in John 14, where He said, *"Greater works then these you will do because I go to the Father. Whatever you ask in My name, that I will do, so that the Father may be glorified in the Son."*

## Prophet

A prophet has a passion for repentance and restoration. Prophets, in the New Testament, are described simply as *"one who speaks to men for edification and exhortation and consolation. Prophecy is a sign, not to unbelievers but to those who believe."* What is the purpose of the prophet? 1 Corinthians 14 tells us that in prophecy the secrets of the heart are disclosed, or illuminated, *"so he will fall on his face and worship God, declaring that God is certainly among you."* How does the prophet operate? In 2 Peter 1:21 we see that *"no prophecy was ever made by an act of human will, but men moved by the Holy Spirit spoke from God."*

## Evangelist

An evangelist has a passion for lost souls. Evangelists, in 2 Timothy 4, are defined as those who preach the word, are ready in season and out of season: reprove, rebuke, exhort, with great patience and instruction, are sober in all things, and endure hardship. Evangelists are needed because, according to 2 Peter 3, *"The Lord is not slow about His promise, as some count slowness, but is patient toward you not wishing for any to perish but for all to come to repentance."* How then does the evangelist operate? As Paul described, *"I planted, Apollos watered, but God was causing the growth. So, neither the one who plants nor the one who waters is anything, but God who causes the growth."*

## Pastor

A pastor has a passion for cultivating God's children. What does a pastor do? Jeremiah 3:14 describes it concisely: *"Then I will give you shepherds after my own heart, who will feed you on knowledge and understanding."* How does a pastor operate, and why is a pastor needed? 1 Corinthians 2 summarizes it nicely: *"I was with you in weakness and in fear and in much trembling and my message and my preaching were not in persuasive words of wisdom, but in demonstration of the Spirit and of power, so that your faith would not rest on the wisdom of men, but on the power of God."*

## Teacher

A teacher has a passion for Scriptural instruction. What does a teacher do? A teacher delivers instruction for the purpose of showing love from a pure heart and a good conscience and a sincere faith. Why? *"For some men, straying from these things, have turned aside to fruitless discussion, wanting to be teachers of the law, even though they do not understand either what they are saying or the matters about which they make confident assertions"* 1 Timothy 1:5-7. This is only one of many reasons why teachers are needed. How does this all work? 1 Corinthians 2:12,13 tells us that we have received the Spirit who is from God *"so that we may know the things freely given to us by God, which things we speak, not in words taught by human wisdom, but in those taught by the Spirit, combining spiritual thoughts spiritual words."*

### The Model of Spiritual Roles

Where were these spiritual roles modeled? Individuals all throughout Scripture lived out these roles in varying capacities, but these roles culminated in Jesus himself. Jesus lived out each one of these roles for the Body:

**Apostle**—*"Therefore, holy brothers, partakers of a heavenly calling, consider Jesus, the apostle and high priest of our confession..."* Hebrews 3:1

**Prophet**—*"And they took offense at him. Jesus said to them, "a prophet is not without honor except in his hometown and among his own relatives and in his own household."* Mark 6:3, 4

**Evangelist**—*"From that time, Jesus began to preach and say, "Repent, for the kingdom of heaven is at hand."* Matthew 4:17

**Pastor**—*"When Jesus went ashore, he saw a large crowd, and he felt compassion for them because they were like sheep without a shepherd; and he began to teach them many things."* Mark 6:34

**Teacher**—*"Rabbi, we know that you have come from God as a teacher; for no one can do the signs that you do unless God is with him"* John 3:2.

As we look at Jesus and how he lived out these roles, one thing begins to be clear; there may be overlap between roles. In the teacher role, Jesus is praised for his signs and wonders. In the pastor role, Jesus taught the people. This reveals a very interesting characteristic of living out our design; we were designed and gifted to fulfill a primary role, but there may be overlap into areas outside of our gifting where we will have to operate out of our weakness.

# Being Christ-like

When we talk about being "Christ-like," aren't we usually talking about sinning less? This begs the question, "Did Jesus concern Himself with managing sin all day long? Or, did He focus on the mission that He was sent here for?" I propose that being Christ-like may have much more to do with us living out the mission that we were put here for.

*"And we know that God causes all things to work together for good to those who love God, to those who are called according to the will of God. For those whom he foreknew, he also predestined to be, conformed to the image of his son, so that he would be the firstborn among many brothers; and these who he predestined, he also called; and these whom he called, he also justified; and these would be justified, he also glorified. What then shall we say to these things? If God is for us, who is against us?" Romans 8:28-31.*

We Christians have heard this passage so many times that we blow right through it, and some of us only hear a particular theological stance in these words. If this is the case, then we are missing a very special element of our story as God's children. First of all, when the word *predestined* is used, many people instantly assume it is talking about "salvation." I believe this is a very limiting explanation of this verse. When I read the word, *predestined,* I see a beautiful promise of destiny: God-designed destiny. Interestingly, many Christians get hung up on this idea of a special destiny and really have a hard time accepting it. They simply do not believe they are worthy of the calling. If they were to dig deeper in this passage however, they would see that it is not their definition of worth that applies here. It reads that not only are we predestined, we are called, we are justified, and here it is—we are glorified! He glorified us! What does this mean? To glorify means to cause the dignity and worth of some person or thing to become manifest and acknowledged. God says we are worthy of the role he called us to fill. Period.

What can keep us from realizing our Spiritual Role as determined by our Creator? I believe there are 5 main deterrents:

1. You may not know what you are passionate about
2. You may still be believing lies from the enemy, designed expressly to keep you from believing you have a special identity in Christ.
3. You may feel guilt over not having a passion for certain roles (roles that are not yours to fill)
4. You may acknowledge that Jesus Christ died to pay for your sin, but you still hold onto the guilt and shame of it.
5. You are on the "hamster wheel" of duty, trying to "repay" Jesus for what He freely and completely conquered!

# Conclusion

We were predestined for an abundant life; a life full of empowerment and authority, one of intimacy and communion with our Maker. We know this at our core, but so many of us endure a lifetime of religion without ever experiencing the fulfillment that God intends for us. Through intimacy with our Father, He reveals who He is and who we are, and invites us into our role in His kingdom.

# Chapter ten

# True Identity:
# Spiritual Gifts

The following morning, Jonet and Jonathan stood prepared for their assignment. Both had their armor strapped on. Each one bore their weapons. And the king's crest was pinned over their hearts for all to see. Nervous anticipation caused them to fidget as they awaited Donatella.

"Good morning, children," she exclaimed upon arrival. "Are we ready for the day?" "We are," asserted Jonathan, even though his hands shook enough to cause him to grip his javelin tightly, so it wouldn't be noticeable.

"Young ones, I have something else to give you before you begin," said Donatella, as she reached out tenderly and placed her hands upon the top of Jonet's head. "To you, Jonet, I give my mercy—you have felt, and will continue to feel, the hearts of others. This ability will guide you as to how to reach out to them, and I will let you know whose time it is for you to engage with. I also give you my peace, so that you may comfort those who I lead you to."

"And upon you, Jonathan, I bestow the gift of knowledge. With it, you will be able to identify the target—the pin-pointed objective—the root issue, and I will help you understand how to engage with it. I also give you the ability to see what others do not." And with this, she placed within his breast pocket a pair of spectacles. "These are not for now, but later," she added.

Donatella escorted the two children, who were definitely a little taller by now, down a corridor to a room they had not seen before. There were charts hanging on the wall and a map was spread across a giant table in the center of the room. Proto was there, standing over the map, and moving figurines around upon its surface.

"Ah, Jonet. Jonathan. Come in," he directed. "Take a seat." "Good morning, judge!" called out Jonathan. "Here, in this room, I am not the judge," replied Proto. "My role *here* is commander. Listen now, for we need to review your assignment." And using the map, Proto—the commander—took the time to explain the great campaign that he was waging on behalf of his father, the king. In the center of the map stood the kingdom. In some locations, a great stone wall (like the one they had crossed under) separated the kingdom from the outside. Other edges had mountain or ocean, and in some cases, even small villages.

Proto focused in on the portion of the map where the gate to the Orphans' Forest stood. "Jonathan. Jonet." Proto leaned in toward them. "I am sending you on a mission into the heart of the forest. There are so many fatherless children there, and to pursue only one or two at a time isn't good enough. I want to take the whole forest! Your mission is to find the source—the cause—of abandonment, and end it."

Proto continued. "You know that forest better than anyone, and I know that you care about the people left behind there. Your eyes have since been opened to the nefarious tendrils and tentacles that keep children entangled there. Jonathan. Jonet. Will you accept this mission?"

Needless to say, the two agreed to the task—although, they didn't really understand what the task *actually* was. What would they be doing, exactly? They hadn't really been told any specifics.

"Will Donatella be guiding us," asked Jonet, confident that she knew the answer. "Yes, sister," assured Commander Proto. "Yes, she will. Come now. I am sending you out as soldiers under my command. Donatella will relay my directions to you. I will remain here in the command center, orchestrating all the troops, but with her guidance and wearing your royal crest displayed on your heart, equipped in your armor and weaponry, you are prepared for the mission."

Donatella escorted the two young soldiers through the city and to the forest gateway. "Remember, I am with you," reassured Donatella. "I will instruct you along the way."

The two of them must have been quite the sight to the other children, who definitely felt smaller to Jonathan and Jonet. They strode through the Fields of Entanglement, their custom-fitted armor nearly effortless to move about in. Jonet bore her ornate dagger within her belt, and Jonathan walked along using the flat end of his javelin as a walking staff. And soon enough, they entered the canopy of the Orphans' Forest.

Nothing looked out of place. Old familiar footpaths lay before them. Shelters perched among the trees. Rustling trees cast mottled shadows on the forest floor. So, the two siblings proceeded cautiously, but without knowing what exactly they were looking for, it felt more like wandering. They finally reached the far side of the forest, which ended at a cliff face. Somewhat bewildered, Jonathan turned to Jonet. "I don't understand. Did you see anything?" "No, I didn't. I thought for sure we would have found *something* by now."

Just then, Donatella's voice sounded in Jonathan's ear. "Jonathan. Pull out the spectacles you were given, and put them on. You will need them from here." He had nearly forgotten about the glasses, but he reached inside his breast pocket, gently pried them open, and slipped them on."

His eyes took a few moments to acclimate to the change in lighting, but suddenly, he jumped, and pulled the spectacles off. Back on. Off again. Jonathan could not believe his eyes. "What is it? What are you seeing?" asked the startled Jonet. "It—it—it's like a different world! I mean, I can still see the forest, but, I see so much more! There are colors, and swirls, and," turning to Jonet, he added, "and it almost seems like I can faintly see Donatella here with us!" "Here, let me see!" exclaimed Jonet.

"Soldiers! There is no time to delay! We must move forward," came Donatella's voice. "Jonathan, you will lead the way from here. Look around you for the clues." Jonathan slowly turned, in small degrees, until he had rotated all the way around in a circle. He paused as he faced the cliff face. "Jonet," he whispered. "Jonet, this isn't a cliff at all! This is a dark castle standing before us! How did we never see this before?"

Donatella guided them forward until they came upon a doorway into the castle. The two peered around the corner and into the castle, and despite feeling uneasy about their surroundings, Donatella's voice brought comfort. "Soldiers, let's move forward."

Jonathan began to notice a strange bluish glow emanating from somewhere inside the stone passageways. "Take the stairs up," directed Donatella. Jonathan led Jonet as they quietly made their way up the stone staircases to the highest point of the castle—and they perched themselves there atop the rampart. It was from this vantage point that Jonathan first saw the dragon. And while Jonet couldn't *see* anything, she began to *feel* that something was definitely not right.

"Something's coming," whispered Jonathan. "I know—I can sense it," Jonet replied. Jonathan peered over the edge of the fortified wall, down into the castle courtyard below. Engulfed in a translucent, blueish glow, a creature crawled slowly. It must have been a strange sight for Jonathan, for it looked like a cross between a crocodile and an iguana. As he squinted his eyes to try to see better, he saw that the dragon was carrying a basket it its mouth, its teeth gripping the handle as it swung along beneath its jaw. There, curled up inside the basket, was a child. Jonathan was instantly enraged.

From Jonet's perspective, they had scaled the cliff face and were now sitting atop the great rock wall, where, to the right, she could see over the forest and the field, across to King Avinu's city. Over to the left, she could see the far side of the king's realm, and one of the villages at the eastern side. Jonathan was also looking this direction, through the lenses of his spectacles. And what he saw explained so much. From the village far in the distance, the dragon was stealing children and taking them to the Orphans' Forest. *It* was the one populating the grove. *It* was the one replenishing the food. It all made sense now. And Jonathan was determined to rescue the orphans. The dragons *had* to be stopped.

Jonet couldn't see the dragon, but she could see a child moving through the castle courtyard toward the gateway to the forest. "Jonathan, aim your javelin right behind the dragon's ear—there's a soft spot there. Jonet, as soon as he launches his javelin, I want you to run down to the child. Jonathan—go NOW!" directed Donatella.

Jonathan stood to his feet and raised the javelin, and threw it down into the castle courtyard with all his might. His aim was true, and it pierced the dragon deep into its soft spot. It shrieked and writhed and dropped the basket from its mouth as it fled through the passages and into the distance. Jonet, of course, was right there with the child, who awoke in all the commotion. The child had been bound with the same tendrils that Jonet had first seen in the Fields of Entanglement, and she knew what to do. With one hand, she soothed the child, and with the other, she pulled her dagger and gingerly sliced away the fibers that wrapped so tightly around.

Jonathan was relieved and surprised it was all over so quickly. Nonetheless, they had vanquished the dragon and rescued the child. The two young soldiers knew that it was best to take the shortest path back through the forest, across the field, and through the trap door into the city. As they emerged from the forest, and into the field, however, Jonet again felt the same as before in the castle—that something was very wrong. "Jonathan, do you see anything? Is something following us?" He turned around and peered through the spectacles into the dark forest. "No, nothing's there. I don't see anything." But as they made their way toward the center of the field, he took one last look behind. The same eerie blue glow he had seen around the dragon seemed to be lighting up the forest—increasingly—as far as he could see to the left and to the right. "Jonet..." He didn't have time to finish his thought, because just then, a dragon—much larger than the first—leaped from the forest cover, and smaller ones followed behind. "Run!!!" he shrieked, and as fast as they could possibly move, they cleared the remaining distance to the trap door, jumped inside, and slammed the lid shut. Jonet was gripped with an ominous dread, and Jonathan was terrified. They hurried through the tunnel and back into the safety of the city.

When Donatella met them at the gate, she tended to the three of them. "Peace to both of you," she spoke as she rested her hands on their heads. "I will take the child from here, you two. Now, make your way back to the commander to debrief."

Proto welcomed them with rousing congratulations. "I am so proud of you both! Well done! It pleases me greatly when you follow my directions, even when you don't understand the whole picture."

"Commander Proto, I thought there was only one dragon, but—we barely escaped from a much larger one! And there were so many!" exclaimed Jonathan.

"Yes, yes there are. And they do nothing but steal, kill and destroy. They are truly despicable creatures. But not to worry. We are victorious. And now, my young soldiers, it is time for you to rest and replenish. Don't fret—
I have soldiers fighting on other fronts as you recover from your mission."

## Reading between the lines

In our story, the Holy Spirit gives Jonet the gift of Mercy, and Jonathan the gift of Knowledge and Discerning of spirits. Jonet is endued with the ability to feel what others are experiencing, while Jonathan can perceive what the heart-of-the-matter, or the root issue, is. He also has the ability (represented by the spectacles) to see into the spiritual realm when the timing is right. The weapons of the two young Christians are directly related to their gifts. Jonet's small dagger of Mercy requires that she be in close contact in order to use it. Jonathan's javelin of Knowledge can be launched from a distance.

Jonet is directed—in a moment of crisis—to pull out her weapon and cut the ties that bind her brother. Jonet has a gift that operates as supernatural *empathy*, and a characteristic of this gift is that she is "in the trenches" with the person needing rescue. She feels what he is experiencing, and as a result, she can intervene on his behalf, as though it were happening to her. She is the proverbial Medic and has to get into close quarters, and that means that she runs a greater risk of being harmed herself. And so, God teams her up with someone with long range attack. Jonathan, with his javelin to hurl from a distance, is *the sniper*.

Jonathan and Jonet are led by the Spirit and both employ their gifting under the direction and empowerment of the Holy Spirit. And as they both follow instruction from the Lord, they accomplish His will and agenda out in the world.

Both of them walk away from the encounter with new understandings. First, they finally understand the true origin of the exploitation and entanglement that entraps mankind—the enemy. And second, they learn that this enemy actively pursues them when they begin to be about their Father's business.

## You have been outfitted for the King's missions

So many Christians are confused about spiritual gifts, and it is no wonder. Denominations define gifts differently, and therefore, try to implement them differently. With so much inconsistency across the board in the practice (or denial) of gifts, we have become really fragmented in this vital area of the Holy Spirit's activity. And, being fragmented, the Body of Christ is disjointed and does not function at its full capacity and potential.

Some Christians are introduced to the gifts of the Spirit with a Scantron form and test questions. In this context, gifts are often intellectualized and reduced down to an academic understanding that can be tabulated by a computer. There is no power and no need for authority here. The gifts are simply perceived as extensions of innate characteristics—sort of like a personality test. A person doesn't have to "work at" or "exercise" their personality, it just "is," and so behave the gifts.

Other Christians are taught that the gifts that require "more" of the Holy Spirit do not exist anymore. In other words, gifts like "service" still exist today, but ones like "healing" do not. "Service" apparently does not depend much on the Holy Spirit; it is an activity that requires *my* effort and discipline. "Healing" depends entirely on the Holy Spirit, and He must not be very interested in drawing unnecessary attention to Himself, according to that viewpoint.

Still others have observed the gifts, particularly the "sign" gifts—gifts like miracles, prophecy, and healing, practiced in a way that is disorderly, comical, purpose-less, and confusing, and are deeply concerned that this display is not inspired by God, much less empowered by Him. And regardless, if it were, why would anyone want to subject themselves to these theatrics?

What is a spiritual gift? It is an ability that is pre-designed by God and empowered at His discretion through His children, with supernatural function for the furtherance of the Kingdom of God. Gifting is often seen in a recurring pattern in the life of a believer. If spiritual roles are "what" we are here to do, then spiritual gifts are "how" we are to do it.

Most Christians are familiar with the list of gifts found in the Scriptures. Romans 12 and 1 Corinthians 12 are two passages that speak of gifting: Prophecy, service, teaching, exhortation, giving, leadership, mercy, word of knowledge, word of wisdom, faith, healing, miracles, discernment, tongues, and interpretations. Is this a complete list? Some say yes, and others say no. Some would add artistic ability to this list, as described in Exodus 31 and 35. Others would add strength to this list, as in the story of Samson in Judges 13-16; after all, it was a recurring ability that was empowered by the Spirit of God. And some would add celibacy as a gift that requires supernatural enabling. We won't go into detailed descriptions of all the gifts here, as we have already covered this in our previous book, "The Holy Spirit of the Bible."

## Designed to be heroes

One of my favorite movies is "Unbreakable," by M. Night Shyamalan. It is the story of the emergence of a hero. The antagonist in the movie is played by Samuel

L. Jackson, who owns an art gallery. He has a theory that I believe fits the Christian story perfectly.

"I've come to believe that comics are our last link to the ancient way of passing on history. The Egyptians drew pictures on walls about battles and events. Countries all around the world still pass on knowledge through pictorial forms. I believe that comics, just at their core now...have a truth. They are depicting what someone, somewhere, felt or experienced. Then of course that core got chewed up in the commercial machine and gets jazzed up, made titillating—cartooned for the sale rack."

I believe that the authentic, empowered, authoritative work of the Holy Spirit through gifts is where comic books got their original inspiration. Bear with me here. Where would the concept of super-strength come from? Samson; he was the first person in recorded history with super-strength. What about the ability to call down fire? Elijah. Sure, it is possible that some of the comic book characters were inspired by occultic ability, but if anything the enemy comes up with is simply a rip-off of God's original design, then ultimately the inspiration would have to be credited again to God!

What is the point we are making here? For the Christian, your gifts are superpowers! All Christians have some combination, after all, as seen in 1 Corinthians 12:7, *"But to each one is given the manifestation of the Spirit for the common good."*

What young boy didn't grow up daydreaming about being a hero, or better yet, a superhero! I believe that we "relate" with specific superheroes for very telling reasons; we often have great similarities! I will go out on a limb here and say that I believe the daydreams we have as children are often directly related to our specific wiring and to the gifting that will eventually emerge in us.

When my boyhood friends and I would "compare notes" about what super-power we would wish for, they would mention flight, invisibility, and the sort, but my answer was always the same—I wanted super-strength. My favorite super-hero was always Wolverine. He is a brute. He is hairy-chested and manly. His skeleton is unbreakable. And, unlike those other superheroes with ranged powers (the ability to fight from a distance), Wolverine had to fight hand-to-hand. But, Wolverine is not all brawn, he is a brooding, pensive character who exhibits great leadership and wise mentoring, but prefers to be alone with his thoughts. Wolverine is the "warrior-poet" of the superhero world. I cannot begin to describe to you how much I relate with this character.

What about you? Which superhero did you relate with, and why? If superhero abilities are, in fact, inspired by how the Spirit of God operates, which ability resonates most with you? Comic books call them by names like empathy, omnilingualism, and vitakinesis; the Scriptures call them by names like mercy, interpretations, and healing. Precognition is prophecy, and clairaudience is a type of discernment.

Before we head too far off into this analogy, let's bring it all back to Scripture, which is very clear about how this all works. It is not about us! Ephesians 1:16-20 illuminates this a bit for us:

*What—Apostle Paul prays that the "Father of Glory may give to you a spirit of wisdom (word of wisdom) and of revelation (prophecy) in the knowledge of Him. I pray that the eyes of your heart may be enlightened (discernment)...*

*Why—So that you will know what is the hope of His calling, what are the riches of the glory of His inheritance in the saints, and what is the surpassing greatness of His power toward (Greek: eis=INTO) us who believe.*

*How—These are in accordance with the working of the strength of His might which He brought about in Christ, when He raised Him from the dead and seated Him at His right hand in the heavenly places..."*

Let me sum up this passage; the Father gives the gifts so that we will have hope regarding the destiny He designed us for, and so that we will experience His incredible power in us, the same power that He used to reanimate the body of Jesus!

What is *our* role in this process? A central response that we are to have to God is stated in Ephesians 6:17, the famous "armor of God" passage, *"Take the helmet of salvation, and the sword of the Spirit, which is the word of God."* Ok. Got it. Take the sword of the Spirit. Check. What does this mean? How do I take up this sword?

## How does it work?

Hebrews 4:12 provides some insight here. The sword of the Spirit is the word of God. "For the word of God (Greek=logos) is living and active and sharper than any two-edged sword, and piercing as far as the division of soul and spirit of both joints and marrow, and able to judge the thoughts and intentions of the heart."

The word of God is *Logos*. Logos means *a word spoken by a living voice, what has been spoken*, and *the act of speaking*. In other words, the word of God is expected to be live, current, and happening now. Of course, the definition also includes written Scripture, but the Greek word implies that someone is speaking. The word of God is His voice. The word of God, that razor-sharp sword of the Spirit, is His live voice speaking into my heart.

You see, this is how gifting operates. God speaks; we listen and obey. God directs; we follow. God invites; and we join Him. Doing the will of the Father often boils down to listening for His prompting and taking action on it.

## Proper perspective on gifts

So, based on this rationale, gifting begins to take a back-seat to the greater focus, which is the will of God. God's agenda, His business, will dictate how and when He enables gifting. So, our obsession need not be about what gifts we have, but rather about hearing our Father and responding to Him. If He prompts me to introduce myself to a particular person and pray for their healing, I do not need to assess my gifts to see if I have this in my arsenal. What I do need to do is take the step of faith in obeying Him, and leave the results up to Him. If He uses me to heal someone, that may mean I have the gift of healing, or it may simply mean He empowered that gift through me just for that moment.

It is our role in this process to obey His leading, and to do so expecting His empowerment, and to rejoice in giving Him credit for the results. 1 Peter 4:10-11 summarizes this nicely, *"As each one has received a gift, employ it in serving one another as good stewards of the manifold grace of God; whoever speaks, as the oracles (mouthpiece) of God; whoever serves, as one who is serving by the strength which God supplies; so that in all things God may be glorified through Jesus Christ, to whom belongs the glory and dominion forever and ever. Amen."*

The Holy Spirit does not need to wait for Christians to gather in a church service for Him to empower and utilize the gifts, as seems to be the assumption of some. He may provide you with a word of knowledge for the person standing in line with you at the grocery store. He may inspire you to give a bag of food to a family whose need has gone unnoticed. He may empower your discernment to understand what is going on in the unseen realm in order to know how to pray during a crisis. The use of the gifts is intended to advance the kingdom of God, and to build up the Body of Christ. It is not intended to be concentrated, once a week in a Sunday morning worship service, with everyone practicing the same gift at once.

## Conclusion

What can we expect to happen when we live this way? Spiritual maturity happens. Hebrews 5:14 touches on this as we read, *"Solid food belongs to those who are mature, that is, for those who by reason of practice have exercised their senses to discern between good and evil."* As we practice, in this case, discernment through all our senses, we mature. Isn't that the quest that many of us are on: the quest for maturity in Christ? Well, here is the answer!

Are you living in denial of the gifting that God has designed within you? If so, you are asleep on the job. *"Awaken, sleeper, and arise from the dead, and Christ will shine on you. Therefore, be careful how you walk, not as unwise men but as wise, making the most of your time, because the days are evil. So then do not be foolish, but understand what the will of the Lord is. And do not get drunk with wine, for that is dissipation, but be filled with the Spirit..."* (Ephesians 5:14-18).

In other words, Wake up!!! Be wise! Make the most of your time here! Time is short! Understand what God's agenda is, and by the way, don't be stupid. Don't waste your time, looking to "feel" something through self-medication. Instead, be filled with the Spirit.

# Chapter eleven

## Identity Theft: Your True Name

Jonathan and Jonet enjoyed a long rest upon completion of the mission. They dined in the king's house—which, of course, was now *their* house. They strolled through the cobblestone alleys of his great kingdom, and soon made fast friends with many of his people. They spoke with other, older citizens of the city, and exchanged stories of the missions they had returned from.

One morning, as they sat reading before the fireplace within the great library, Avinu entered in, as was his custom in the early hours of the day. He quietly sat between the two and spread his arms out along the back of the tufted couch. Jonet instinctively slouched to the side and leaned into him as she continued reading. Jonathan remained as he was, but he turned his whole body toward Avinu, and began asking him questions about his kingdom, but mostly just about his thoughts on things. And after some time, Avinu shifted the conversation to something else that was on his mind.

"Jonet. Jonathan. Do you remember anything from before your life in Orphans' Forest?" They shook their heads. "No, Avinu, that is as far back as we can remember. We had just always been there—we didn't know there was anything before that," spoke Jonathan. "Well, young ones," said Avinu, "I would like to tell you a little about where you come from."

"You come from the village on the eastern end of my kingdom. It is a place where *some* people are loyal subjects of mine, but many others live in rebellion against me. Instead of banishing the rebels just yet, I make every attempt to win them over, and even if they refuse me, I try to win over their children."

"I first met you two when you were still in your mother's womb. You, my dears, were twins. I had come across your pregnant mother out in the marketplace of your village. She acted like she didn't know who I was, and I didn't intrude. But I did speak a blessing over you both that day, and I spoke my very first invitation to you to join me in my kingdom. I knew you could hear me—even in the womb— and I could see you jump and kick for joy at the promises I spoke over you. I told you then and there that I wanted you—that I was choosing you—and since Donatella was with me, I told her to keep an eye on you both."

Jonathan and Jonet were stunned and didn't quite know what to say. After a moment, Jonathan blurted out, "So, we really are brother and sister? In real life?" Avinu smiled and nodded. "And we have a mother?" Jonet added.

"Yes, dear. You do."

"You *wanted* us?" It was the most wonderful thing they had ever heard.

"I wanted you, yes, and I came back to visit you when you were born! The good news of your birth brought me back, and when I arrived, I brought gifts and qualities, strengths and passions, and I instilled them within you, so they could never be taken from you. And with my finger, I touched your forehead and left my imprint upon you—an imprint that is not visible to the naked eye. It can only be perceived in the unseen realm—the realm that Jonathan sees when he puts on his spectacles."

"The dragons you saw sneak into that very village, and they hunt the children that bear my imprint upon them. They try to steal them, wipe their memory, implant labels and lies, and hide them from me in the Orphans' Forest. That, of course, is where your memories begin."

"But did you know, Jonathan and Jonet, that when I blessed you and imprinted you, that I also gave you a royal name? You, Jonathan, have always been known in *my* household as Valiant Vanguard, for you are courageous and you are wired to be like the tip of a spear—striking with precision." Jonathan was stunned to hear such illustrious words about himself, and he could hardly choke back the tears. He simply looked up at Avinu with watery eyes, and nodded.

"And you, daughter, your true name is Sarah Strong. For you are my princess, and you have an incredible strength within you—especially to rescue those who need someone in the danger beside them." A smile crept to Jonet's lips. "I am strong?" she asked sheepishly. "So, so strong, my princess," Avinu replied.

There were so many questions left unanswered, and Avinu knew this. But there would be many more conversations to come, so he directed them to visit Proto the next day in the command center, for a new mission awaited the newly christened *Valiant* and *Sarah*. The two spent the rest of the day daydreaming about their royal identities and finally went to sleep, their hearts delighted and their minds aflutter.

The following day, Proto welcomed them into his command center and explained their next mission. They were to go back into Orphans' Forest and rescue more children. "But Proto," voiced Jonathan, "What about the dragons! There were so many!" "Valiant," replied Proto (who refused to call him Jonathan any longer), "Valiant, I have given you weapons. I have given you the king's crest as a badge. You have Donatella's voice to guide you. Nevertheless, I will be with you as well.

If you find yourself overwhelmed, call upon me and I will be there." Jonathan and Jonet—Valiant and Sarah—were understandably concerned, but they agreed and proceeded nervously to the forest gate. They lifted the trap door, ever so slightly, and peeked out—across the Field of Entanglement and toward the Orphans' Forest. Sarah once again felt the creepy sensation that she had when they were last here, and Valiant—having put on his spectacles—despondently confirmed that the forest still glowed with an evil blue light. The dragons were certainly there. "I don't know about this," said Sarah. "Me neither," replied Valiant, "but Commander Proto did seem to have this all planned out. I believe him. We will be ok." And with this assertion, Valiant raised the trap door open, and before Sarah even knew what was happening, he had pulled her up and into the field.

To their amazement, all the way to the left, and equally to the right of them were lined up other citizens of the kingdom, dressed in armor, with their badges pinned to their chests and their weapons drawn. Some carried swords of all different shapes and sizes. Others carried bows and arrows. Still others had battle-axes, maces and hatchets. Everyone was ready for their mission. And after what seemed like an eternity of silence, Donatella's voice marked the start of the mission, and everyone took a step forward toward the small children who were still rummaging in the field and had not yet taken notice of the soldiers.

It was at this moment that the first of the dragons emerged from the cover of the forest. And the soldiers who wore spectacles saw them and began their attack. Spears, javelins and arrows flew. And as more dragons appeared in the clearing, even more soldiers ran toward them with axes and swords and engaged in the fight. But Valiant had not thrown his javelin, for, contrary to reason, Donatella had told him to wait. So, poised and ready, he remained watchful and wary.

Some soldiers remained active on the communicators, relaying messages from the commander. Others ran through the field announcing the king's purpose and inviting the children into the walled city. Sarah found herself, and others like her, with daggers drawn, cutting the children free from the grip of the tendrils that continued to wrap around their feet and legs.

Valiant felt useless as he observed his fellow soldiers in the field—that is, until he laid his eyes upon *the great dragon*—the one that dwarfed all the others. "This, Valiant, is yours," came Donatella's voice. "Ready your javelin!"

It was as if the great dragon knew that Valiant had him in his sights, for it began scurrying—the way lizards do—directly toward him, and at a speed that caught Valiant off-guard. It was hard to get a good angle as he aimed once more for the soft spot behind the ear. "Hold…hold…" came Donatella's voice in his ear. "NOW Valiant!"

It was as though time had slowed, and all sound drained from his ears. With a running start, the javelin launched into the air, flexing and bending as it cut its way through the thick atmosphere of conflict.

As it pierced the vulnerable hide behind the great dragon's ear, the javelin plunged deep. The scaled lizard reeled to one side, and desperately clawed at the javelin, but its anger must have been stronger than the pain, for it fastened its gaze upon Valiant and began to charge once more. And unprepared for this, Valiant froze in fear.

The dragon leaped upon him and pinned him to the ground, sinking its claws deep within his shoulder, just above his heart. Valiant grasped at the javelin, but he couldn't quite reach it. And as he lay there helpless—the other soldiers engaged in their own skirmishes—the dragon dug its claws deeper into his flesh and dangerously close to his heart. With the last bit of breath he could muster, Valiant screamed out "Proto!!! Help me!" And with this, his head slumped to the side and the dragon lowered its jaws to feast on its prey.

It was hard for Sarah to describe what she observed at this point in the story. Suddenly the sky flashed white, and all sound seemed to drain from the air, except for a ringing in the ears. Beyond the brightness, and through squinted eyes, she could make out the form of Proto, mounted on a horse, and flying over the battle in a leap that seemed unending. His sword was drawn, but he didn't appear to need it.

Everyone's badges began beaming the same white light—including Valiant's, and it shot up from his chest, penetrating the head of the great dragon. The lizard reeled up and contorted, then began an extended fall as it slumped to the ground beside Valiant.

When the brilliance of the light finally waned, and people once again became recognizable, Jonet watched Proto alight from his horse, bend down and say something to Valiant, who was laying on the battlefield. Proto took him by the hand, raised him to his feet, and walked him toward Jonet and the other soldiers who had begun to gather round.

"Brother and sisters," proclaimed Proto, "I am so proud of you all. You fought well today. We are victorious in defeating the dragon menace, but we still have orphans to rescue. Now, I want you to watch me and do exactly what I do. Hear me, and say exactly what you hear me say."

Commander Proto turned back toward the city wall, lifted his right hand, and thrust it toward the wall. His left hand then extended toward the Orphans' Forest. "Repeat this with me now soldiers!" called Proto. "On behalf of the great King Avinu Malkeinu, I claim this field and forest for the kingdom. Nevermore shall it be the territory of darkness, nor the domain of dragons. Henceforth this land will be called the King's Forest, and it will be home to light and life." And with these words, Proto again thrust his right hand toward the wall, and motioned for the others to do the same. "To this wall—I command movement. You will no longer be a barrier for the fatherless. Arise!" Proto motioned his outstretched hand upward, as if lifting a great weight, and all the soldiers followed suit. And, as if it had understood the command and had no choice but to obey, the great wall slowly lifted from the ground, responding to the outstretched hands and commanding voices. Proto—and the others—raised their right arms and arched them over until the wall had traveled over the field—above the forest—and settled down on the far side, up against the cliffs. The field and forest—now the King's—were completely enclosed, like a nature preserve. Gone were the dragons, and with them, the tendrils that used to keep the orphans in bondage.

"This, brothers and sisters, is something worth celebrating!" shouted Proto. "Now go, round up all the orphans you can find, and bring them into the kingdom. You tell them all that the king has invited them in!"

But as for Valiant and Sarah, Proto led them back toward the city and into the house of the king.

## Reading between the lines

Our Father in heaven designed us and chose us while we were still in our mother's womb. He crafted us in His image, and marked us as His own. Tragically, however, the enemy targets those children the Lord has called His own, and attempts to steal, kill and destroy us in order to prevent us from coming to faith in Jesus Christ. This is the origin of the orphans in our story.

The Father lavishes His approval on Jonet and Jonathan from before their birth, and bestows upon each of them a name of His choosing. These names are the ultimate summary of their identities. Valiant Vanguard: courageous and initiator of action. Sarah Strong: *my* strong princess.

Our two heroes—no longer young children—discover more about themselves at the same time they learn about God. Perhaps a better way to say it is this—God reveals more of Himself and more of our own self—the further we move into maturity.

In our story, Proto (as Jesus) reveals the magnitude of His power and glory when He decimates the dragon enemy and raises Valiant to life on the battlefield.

## Who are you really?

"You are a failure." "You will never amount to anything." "You should be more like your brother." "You are lazy." "You are weird."

Labels can have a powerful impact on our lives. The old saying, *"Sticks and stones may break my bones, but names will never hurt me,"* is simply not true. Labels can be seemingly impossible to shake. Labels define the reality we come to adopt as truth, and they exert an inescapable control over us as we live either affirming the label or struggling against it.

Not all labels are "negative." Some are considered well-meaning, but they can be exploited by our enemy to, once again, control us. "You are beautiful." "You are my 'smart' child." "You are so bubbly!" All of these can become engrained and form ruts in our personhood, ultimately creating a defining cage that traps and oppresses.

In all of these cases and countless more, we are being labeled with adjectives—descriptive words that tell us *how* we are. The trouble is that we take them to define *who* we are as well.

This isn't a new phenomenon. People in the Scriptures endured this same experience. And unfortunately, many times these people bore the labels their entire lives, in the form of their birth name. Nowadays, names are much more innocuous; my name means "hill of broom flowers." Clearly, I do not take this to be a label in my life and I have never tried to live up to my name or live in spite of it—it is just a name. However, in the Scriptures we see parents that were much more deliberate in naming their children. Often, the names they chose or created reflected what the parent was feeling, believing or experiencing about their circumstances or about the future of their child. Hope or trust can be heard in certain names; despair or fear can be heard in others.

If we look up biblical names in Genesius' Hebrew-Chaldee Lexicon, we find the original meanings of many names. Eliezer means *"God of help,"* while Asher means *"happy,"* or *"happy am I!"* Both names seem to reflect a trust in God and a contentment in His blessing. Names, in this spirit, can serve as a powerful blessing that propels a person forward in life.

On the other hand, Perez means *"a breach,"* or *"What a breach you have made for yourself!"* Jacob means *"a supplanter,"* or *"one who follows on another's heels,"* and *"one who takes the credit of another."* Finally, Esau can mean *"red,"* *"hairy,"* or, as in Jewish tradition, *"a doer."* So, let me get this straight about the brothers Esau and Jacob. Esau is a doer, maybe a "hard-worker" would be fair to say, and Jacob, well, he took the credit? Based on what we see in Scripture, they lived up to this, didn't they? Names, in this context, can serve as a curse upon a person, or, to use a more current term, a label.

## God redefines and restores

Here's the good news about labels: God loves to overturn labels! Throughout time, He has redefined the identity and significance of *places, practices, and people.*

God redefines the identity of places. In Joshua 5, we read that Joshua has been circumcising all the sons of Israel at a place that earns the name, Gibeath-haaraloth, which means *"hill of foreskins."* God has a better idea and renames the place with the significant term, Gilgal, *"rolling,"* to commemorate the day that God "rolled away the reproach of Egypt" from them.

He also redefines the identity of practices. In Acts 10, Peter receives a vision in which he is instructed to eat unclean animals, a practice that was strictly forbidden among Jews. So, Peter refuses to eat them. But, God again tells Peter in a vision to eat them, and to no longer call unholy what God has cleansed. This is a huge moment! God shifts the paradigm by having Peter break from Jewish tradition, essentially nullifying the practice and reversing it! Of course, we know what happens next—this act is the catalyst that sends the good news of Jesus Christ out to the Gentiles.

Finally, God redefines the identity of people. In Hosea 1, the prophet has a child whom the Lord instructs him to name, Lo-ammi, *"for you are not My people and I am not your God."* Hosea's family dysfunction represents the back-and-forth relationship between Israel and God; they are a metaphor. Accordingly, later on in Hosea, God brings restoration when He says, *"I will say to those who were not My people, 'You are My people!' And they will say, 'You are my God!'"*

## Biblical characters and their True Identity

All throughout the Bible, God exchanges the old identity of people for His true identity for them. We frequently see a shift in identity when God calls people into their destiny. Here is a partial list of such characters:

- Abram (exalted father) to Abraham (father of a multitude)
- Sarai (my princess) to Sarah (Princess)
- Jacob (one who follows on another's heels) to Israel (one who has power with God and men and prevails)
- James (son of Jacob) and John (Yahweh is gracious) to Boanerges (sons of thunder)
- Joseph (Jehovah increases) to Barnabas (son of encouragement)
- Simon (obedient) to Peter (a mass of rock detached from the living rock)

Peter's story is quite fascinating. In John 1:42, the first time that the Bible records any interaction with him, Jesus reveals to Peter his True Name. *"You are Simon the son of John; you shall be called Cephas (Aramaic for Peter)."* Yet, throughout the next three years, Jesus continues to call him by his natural name, Simon. He occasionally reminds Simon of his True Name. *"Blessed are you, Simon Bar-Jona, because flesh and blood did not reveal this to you, but My Father who is in heaven. I also say to you that you are Peter, and upon this rock I will build My church, and the gates of Hades will not overpower it"* Matthew 16:17,18. At Jesus's last encounter with him, He still called him by his old name. *"Simon, son of John, do you love Me?"* John 21:17. Peter did not become Peter until Acts 2 when he was filled with the Holy Spirit and released into his destiny.

Gideon is another famous example. Gideon is hiding from his oppressors when God shows up and calls him "Mighty Warrior." Of course, Gideon rants and protests, but God assures him and gives him a sign of proof that it really is God who is engaging with him. God then sends him home to "clean house" and get rid of all the idols in his father's home. When he does so, the community condemns him, and his father steps in and pleads his case that Baal alone should be left to punish Gideon. His father then labels his son Jerubbaal, meaning, "Let Baal contend against him." How ironic that at the very time God reveals his true identity to him, the enemy tries to undermine it with a counter-identity.

## The importance of struggle

It is interesting to note that people who receive their True Name from God in the Bible tend to do so through some crisis of faith, some trial, or some other emotionally heavy exchange with God. It is as though God wants us to struggle through the transition from Old Man to New Man, from False Self to True Name. Just like the caterpillar metamorphoses and has to painfully tear its way out of its cocoon, it is the only way it can emerge into its true form—a butterfly. I remember as a boy the story my parents told me about the man who had been watching a cocoon that was hanging under his eaves. The day finally came for the changeling butterfly to emerge from the trappings of its chrysalis, when the man noticed that the trapped butterfly was struggling—essentially scratching and clawing its way out. The man felt great sympathy for the butterfly, and so, as gingerly as he could, he helped open the chrysalis, so the butterfly wouldn't have to struggle. It was only after the butterfly had fully emerged that the truth became clear—the butterfly was unable to fly as a result of his intervention.

God could just magically zap us with these life changing truths, but He seems to be just as interested in the process as He is with the result. In this spirit, He allows—no, He *invites* us to struggle through. Gideon struggled with his new identity; he challenged God, he demanded proof, he questioned, but, he obeyed as well. Jacob wrestled with God; he refused to relent when he was told to "let go." He experienced pain for wrestling with God, but he received the blessing of blessings in the process: His True Name.

God reaffirms three things when He reveals a True Name: His design, His will, and His reward.

*"I have called you by name; you are Mine!"**

*"You will be called by a new name which the mouth of the LORD will designate."†*

*"To him who overcomes, I will give of the hidden manna, and I will give him a white stone, and a new name written on the stone which no one knows but he who receives it."‡*

These passages are all promises! Some are past promises, while others are for the future. Some are to the Israelites of antiquity, others are to Gentiles of the end times.

## Our Father is our Author

As we have seen, God revealed or promised True Names to practices and places, men and women, nations and individuals, both past and future. These names are commemorations of His grand design, His redemptive work and His unimaginable love toward us. When does He reveal our True Name? The pattern seems to reveal the convergence of three elements in our life: Hearing God's voice, Rejecting labels, and Yielding Control to Him. Those three elements seem to be critical to the process. Clearly, if we do not recognize His voice, that precludes our hearing what He wants to reveal to us directly. If we hear His voice, yet have not yet revolted against the entanglements of lies and labels, we don't really need our True Name yet, do we? We are still content with the status quo. And finally, though we may hear Him, and we are fed up with the old life, if we refuse to accept His invitations to yield up the elements of our life that keep us from Him, we will keep ourselves focused on those things instead of Him. We will delay what our hearts crave most from Him.

Is this hard to accept? Do you believe that you were pre-ordained? Do you believe you were pre-consecrated and pre-appointed? Do you believe you were pre-destined? Do you believe you were pre-designed and pre-assigned?

Allow me to paraphrase and condense God's statements into a single paragraph. These are all individual passages that we already popularly use for encouragement and apply to our current circumstances; we already claim each of these promises, so here they are all together.

---

* Isaiah 43:1
† Isaiah 62:2
‡ Revelation 2:17

*"My eyes saw your unformed substance, and in My book I wrote the story that I ordained for you, before it had even begun. Before I formed you in the womb I knew you; before you were born I dedicated you for My sacred purpose; I have appointed you. I have determined the outcome of your story; your destiny, and I have called you. You are My masterpiece, created in Christ Jesus for the adventure and destiny I have crafted especially for you."\**

Do you believe all this? Do you believe that He created you on purpose, intentionally, specially, and that He crafted a destiny for you, and you for it? Do you believe that He designed you with all the traits and gifts necessary for that destiny? Do you believe you are His workmanship? Do you believe that He went to that great extent to design every aspect of your identity and existence, yet He stopped just short of putting His stamp on you, the essence of who He made you to be—your True Name?

Is there a specific scripture reference that says He has a True Name for you and that He will reveal it to you if you ask Him? Is the word Trinity found in the Bible? The answer to both is no. What we are doing is inferring a truth, based on the complete message of the whole Bible. Just as the concept of the Trinity is based on what the Scriptures portray from beginning to end, so is the concept of your True Name.

## Conclusion

We need our True Name. Not only do we need the affirmation of our Father, we need the clarity and direction—the purpose that it brings. This quote by A.W. Tozer sums it up well:
*"One of the greatest tragedies that we find, even in this most enlightened of ages, is the utter failure of millions of men and women to ever discover why they were born. Deny it if you will—and some persons will—but wherever there are humans in this world, there are people who are suffering from a hopeless and depressing kind of amnesia. It forces them to cry out, either silently within themselves or often with audible frustration, "I don't even know why I was born!"†*

When you know who you are because you know who He says you are, you can live with extreme clarity and purpose, joining Him where you know He invites you and passing on things that are distractions. You are released from old labels. You can begin to walk in authority.

---

\* Psalm 139:16-18, Jeremiah 1:5-6, Romans 8:30, Ephesians 1:10
† "Whatever Happened to Worship," by A.W. Tozer

# Chapter twelve

## Spiritual Authority

Proto led Valiant and Sarah into the great house of the king, and as he walked them through a corridor they had not yet explored, it opened up into a cavernous room with stone walls and dark, wooden floors. On the side walls were countless banners with coats-of-arms and family crests, of various colors and patterns. But they all had a central theme—all were reminiscent of the king's crest that they wore pinned above their hearts. At the far end of the room hung a single banner—a large one that covered the entire wall—and it was unmistakable. This was the king's banner.

But this was almost an insignificant thing to make note of, because there, at the end of the room, was the great King Avinu, and he was seated on a throne that was situated on a raised platform. To his right was a second throne, and Proto, as if on cue, strode across the room and seated himself next to the king. King Avinu called to the two siblings, and they approached the throne.

King Avinu arose from his royal throne and stepped down to the two of them. Taking Sarah's calloused hands in his, Avinu looked deep into her eyes. "Daughter, I am so proud of you! Once again, you have proven yourself." Avinu stepped over to Valiant, and he gently took his stubbled face in his hands. "Son, you were so brave today. I am so pleased with you!"

"Valiant and Sarah, I have watched you grow up into the strong and brave young adults that stand here before me today. We have had many wonderful conversations together by the fireplace in the library. You have been faithful and follow instructions well, and you have completed many missions on my behalf. Well done, good and faithful citizens!"

"Furthermore, you two are a good team. You work well together and complement each other nicely. Since you have been faithful with the small missions Proto has given you, I am going to reward you both. I am giving you two a promotion, if you choose to look at it that way. It comes with honor, but with increased responsibility as well. You have led yourselves well, and now you will lead others."

Upon hearing this, both Valiant and Sarah lowered to their knees. "As you wish, your highness. We would be honored to serve you however you choose," replied Sarah.

The king placed himself deliberately in front of Valiant, and turning back to Proto, he lifted a simple, but golden crown from his hands, and placed it on Valiant's head. "Valiant Vanguard, I declare you a prince of the realm. You are the one who struck the great dragon that enslaved the orphans in my forest. For this reason, I give you the King's Forest to rule on my behalf."

King Avinu stepped over to Sarah, who had her head bowed before him. "Sarah Strong, I declare you a princess of the realm. You freed so many orphans from the grip of the Fields of Entanglement. I now give you these fields to rule on my behalf, and from henceforth, they shall be called the Fruitful Fields. Now, rise, Prince Valiant and Princess Sarah."

"You will be responsible for the protection of the domain I have given you both. Keep it pure. Cultivate it, and make it grow. And as you encounter children in your domain, you are to be my ambassadors. Do you two accept this responsibility?"

"We do, King Avinu," they both replied. Neither one was sure what was appropriate to feel in the moment. Elation? Celebration? Sobriety? Joy? Duty? It didn't matter, because the king's voice put the question to rest. "Come Sarah, come Valiant, I have prepared a banquet in your honor."

Avinu and Proto led them to the banquet room they had seen so long ago but had not yet been invited into. Gathered around the table were all the orphans they had rescued, whose names were on the king's guest list. White tunics flanked the table all around, and there, at the far end of the room, was Donatella, simply beaming. She held out her arms to Valiant and Sarah and called them to their seats of honor. To that date, it was the grandest experience the two siblings ever had. The feast lasted for hours, and when the music was all played, and the food all enjoyed, and the stories all told, Valiant and Sarah slept the deepest, most wonderful sleep of their lives.

From enslaved orphans, to adopted children, to battle-worn soldiers, to prince and princess, the journey had led the two—full-circle—from Freeman's Forest and its deception, to Orphans' Forest and its rescue and redemption, to the King's Forest and the right and responsibility to rule it on the king's behalf.

Who could have known the surreal story—the indescribable destiny—that was unfolding for these two fatherless friends: friends who turned out to be family, both to each other, and ultimately, to the king himself.

## Reading between the lines

Jonathan and Jonet are ushered into the King's throne room—a grand meeting hall where His crest hangs in dramatic display—the same one they wear upon their chest. The massive walls are lined with the coats-of-arms of brothers and sisters in the faith who have gone before them; each crest resembling the King's, but customized with additional insignias to commemorate their missions and fruitfulness.

King Avinu—just like our Father in heaven—honors Valiant Vanguard and Sarah Strong with a crown of achievement, and rewards them by entrusting them to rule small portions of His kingdom.

And finally, the King celebrates them in the great company of those whom they have rescued and ministered to. This is a picture of what legacy can look like in the Kingdom of heaven.

## You have been given authority to act on the King's behalf!

One of the great truths of Scripture that seems to be missing from most pulpits today is one that impacts each one of us every single day. I am speaking of spiritual authority.

What is this authority? Spiritual authority can be described a few different ways: It is our ability to walk in confidence due to a clear sense of our identity as sons and daughters of God; it is boldness to take action, knowing that the Spirit of God is directing and prompting us; and finally, it is a "command presence," knowing how the Spirit of God moves in us and through us to facilitate the things that He prompts us to do.

One of the great stories of authority in the Scriptures is that of David and Goliath. A young Israelite boy, David, hears the villain, Goliath, mocking Yahweh, the God whose name was too holy for the Jews to even mention. David takes action and defeats Goliath. What was the impetus for his action? Was it a great faith that God would show him favor and help him defeat Goliath? Perhaps there was some of that, but when I read the story, I hear the great outrage and righteous indignation that David has toward this villain. His disdain drove him to action. How could he step into that situation? After all, he wasn't a soldier; he was just a shepherd.

David's authority was based on a few things. It was based on his understanding of his weapon: the sling. It was also based on his experience. He had already killed a lion and a bear while tending his father's flock. And finally, it had to do with his heart for God.

Consider two famous fictional characters: Clint Eastwood's "Preacher" from the movie Pale Rider, and Don Knott's "Barney Fife" from the TV series The Andy Griffith Show. Preacher was a man that stood up for what was right, unintimidated by opposition. He needed no weapon—he simply adapted to situations where he knew he needed to step in. Barney Fife, though being a deputy sheriff, and despite having a weapon, was quite the opposite. He was easily intimidated and was constantly trying to prove his power, though it was clear that he did not know how to carry himself in it. Preacher handled himself as though he were wearing a badge; Barney Fife handled himself as though he weren't. When Preacher stepped into a situation, the opposition scurried; when Barney Fife stepped into a situation, the opposition rolled their eyes.

This is, in a small way, what it looks like to walk in authority. In a spiritual context, we are talking about knowing who God is and who you are as a result. I don't mean the churchy language so often heard among Christians, "I am so unworthy, I don't know how God can use me." That is not who you and I are as His children. He has given us our identity, and He has also given us our worth. He considers us worthy because we are His design, and when has His design ever been unworthy? His thoughts toward us should inspire confidence in us, both in relation to our Father in heaven as we as to the forces that oppose us.

*This is the confidence which we have before Him, that, if we ask anything according     to     His     will,     He     hears     us.*

*And if we know that He hears us in whatever we ask, we know that we have the requests which we have asked from Him.*

*For the Father loves the Son, and shows Him all things that He Himself is doing; and the Father will show Him greater works than these, so that you will marvel. 1 John 5:14, 15, 20*

## The Opposite of Authority

Do you feel more like *Barney Fife* than Clint Eastwood's *Preacher*? Barney was fully equipped but had no confidence. The dictionary describes the opposite of authority as laxity.* Spiritually speaking, it is the inability to walk in confidence due to a lack of understanding our identity as sons of God; it is the absence of boldness leading to action, due to unfamiliarity with how the Spirit of God directs and prompts us; and finally, it is a general spinelessness due to lack of understanding how the Holy Spirit moves in us and through us to facilitate the

---

* authority. Thesaurus.com. Concept Thesaurus. Dictionary.com, LLC 2009. http://thesaurus.com/browse/authority (accessed: July 26, 2011).

things He prompts us to do. Have you asked for wisdom in this area? God promises that He will answer!

*But if any of you lacks wisdom, let him ask of God, who gives to all generously and without reproach, and it will be given to him.*

*But he must ask in faith without any doubting, for the one who doubts is like the surf of the sea, driven and tossed by the wind.*

*For that man ought not to expect that he will receive anything from the Lord, being a double-minded man, unstable in all his ways. James 1:5-8*

It is interesting that the last verse of this passage describes a man who is not standing in authority: double-minded (attention split between doubt and faith) and unstable.

## The Model of Authority

What is the action of authority? Authority can become the filter through which we live and operate regularly. As we look at the life of Jesus, we see many examples of how He displayed authority. Jesus cast out demons, healed every kind of disease, displayed power over nature, blessed and cursed, and taught with authority.

When He sent seventy disciples out (not including the twelve), He defined what it would look like for them to walk in authority, and the same framework applies to us:

**They were aligned with His agenda**
(v.1) *"Now after this the Lord appointed seventy others, and sent them in pairs ahead of Him to every city and place where He Himself was going to come.*

**They were active in Kingdom work**
(v.2) *And He was saying to them, "The harvest is plentiful, but the laborers are few; therefore beseech the Lord of the harvest to send out laborers into His harvest.*

**They were guaranteed to have opposition**
(v.3) *"Go; behold, I send you out as lambs in the midst of wolves.*

**They were to have no concern for provision**
(v.4) *Carry no money belt, no bag, no shoes; and greet no one on the way.*

**They were given permission to bless**
(v.5-6) *Whatever house you enter, first say, 'Peace be to this house. If a man of peace is there, your peace will rest on him; but if not, it will return to you.*

**They were to foster fellowship**
(v.7-8) *Stay in that house, eating and drinking what they give you; for the laborer is worthy of his wages. Do not keep moving from house to house. Whatever city you enter and they receive you, eat what is set before you;*

**They were to perform miracles where He directed**
(v.9) *and heal those in it who are sick, and say to them, 'The kingdom of God has come near to you.'*

**They were given permission to curse**
(v.10-11) *But whatever city you enter and they do not receive you, go out into its streets and say, 'Even the dust of your city which clings to our feet we wipe off in protest against you; yet be sure of this, that the kingdom of God has come near.'*

**They were assured power and protection**
(v.19) *Behold, I have given you authority to tread on serpents and scorpions, and over all the power of the enemy, and nothing will injure you.*

**Their identity was reinforced as more significant than results**
(v.20) *Nevertheless do not rejoice in this, that the spirits are subject to you, but rejoice that your names are recorded in heaven."*

**They were allowed to experience God's pleasure in their participation**
(v.21) *At that very time He rejoiced greatly in the Holy Spirit, and said, "I praise You, O Father, Lord of heaven and earth, that You have hidden these things from the wise and intelligent and have revealed them to infants. Yes, Father, for this way was well-pleasing in Your sight."*

Jesus gave these people authority to prepare the way for the kingdom of heaven in advance of His visit. For those who believe that only His twelve closest disciples received such authority, we see that at least seventy others were given this authority as well. And for those who believe that such authority was a result of the Holy Spirit's work at Pentecost in Acts 2, we have to keep in mind that these ancillary disciples wielded this authority long before the Holy Spirit filled those apostles.

As a follow up, Jesus, at the point of His ascension, told all those present, to go make disciples and baptize them, and teaching them to do everything that Jesus instructed.

In August of 2014, I had the incredible privilege to participate in this very act, specifically in regard to my family. Up to that point, I had a growing sense within me that it was time for my young children to be baptized. They had each made a profession of faith already, but we had been waiting for the right moment; and that is exactly what the Lord brought to pass. He had been stirring within me a desire to follow the examples of the jailer* and Lydia†, both of whom had believed in the name of Jesus Christ and converted their whole families, first with declarations of faith, followed by baptism. Sunday, August 24, I baptized my three children in the ocean, and when we gathered afterward as a family on the beach, Desiree and I anointed them with oil, and laid hand on them and prayed for them to receive the Holy Spirit, based on the example in Acts 8:12-17. Finally, we established a covenant between our family and God, dedicating and committing ourselves collectively to Him. It was a wonderful moment, and it reminded me of the significance of Joshua's words, "As for me and my house, we will serve the Lord."‡

The truth is that I would have been way too intimidated previously to consider baptizing my own children. This feeling of inadequacy is, unfortunately, a universal ailment that affects men in the Church. We are often intimidated by the notion of standing in the healthy, biblical capacity that we are each called to. We feel stupid trying to step out in boldness, and so we don't take action. We feel conspicuous trying to lead our families, and so, we allow the brunt of it to default to someone else: our spouse, church, school, etc. But, God is good, who invites us to begin with very small steps and grow into the bolder moments of action.

## Growing in Authority

Authority grows. It is part of the Father's process of bringing us from spiritual adolescence into spiritual maturity.

It all starts back where this book started. We acknowledge, examine, and begin to deconstruct our False Self. We grow in our True Identity: Embracing it and practicing it. We learn what it looks like to yield to our Father, and we begin responding to His invitations to do so in various areas of our lives.

At the point of convergence of Yieldedness, Identity, and Responsiveness, authority begins to grow. Responsiveness is how we obey His promptings. When we have yielded our agendas to Him, embraced our identity and are looking to live it out, and when we start following through on His promptings, we gain some godly experience. Every day we continue in the same manner, the authority grows. Authority is our spiritual backbone. The more experience we get with our Father, the stronger our spine becomes. The more we see Him fulfill His agenda through us, the healthier our spiritual posture becomes. We begin to walk tall because of this confidence we have in how our Father operates.

So, how do we begin to walk in authority? We can begin in our own homes. We can bless ourselves and our families. Blessing is simply speaking God's words of

---

* Acts 16:31-34
† Acts 16:14-15
‡ Joshua 24:15

truth over His children. If we are listening to Him, He will give us the specific words to speak as words of affirmation.

We can identify oppression over ourselves and families and take action against it. Again, if we are listening to our Father, He will direct us on how to take action: what kind of opposition it is, who is being oppressed, which scriptures to speak, etc.

We can "lock-down" our homes every night. Every night I pray over our home—I pray for God's angelic protection around our home, I pray for Him to disallow any demonic activity on our property, and I pray for His presence as we sleep. I verbally claim protection over my family and my domain in the name and authority of Jesus Christ. How many dangers has this lock-down protected us from? We will probably never know. Is it a magical formula that works every single time? No; there are situations where opposition still breaks through and affects our family, and I have to take action.

Another area where we can begin to walk in authority is in the area of our spiritual role: Apostle, Prophet, Evangelist, Pastor, or Teacher. As we live out this aspect of our identity, we listen for the prompting of the Holy Spirit and take action on it. If the Holy Spirit has an agenda and He is directing me to share the gospel with someone or pray over them for healing, I should be able to do so with authority, since He is engineering the encounter. When we walk in authority, we actively look for the work of the Spirit in our surroundings, and we anticipate opportunity to operate in our role everywhere we go and with anyone we are led to.

When you begin to walk in authority, you walk with clarity and focus. Idle time becomes an irritant—you know who you are and you know why you were engineered. To not be living it is to not be alive. In knowing yourself and being led by the Holy Spirit, you begin to filter out the distractions that life is determined to entangle us in. Sometimes the entanglements are sin. Sometimes the entanglements are more subtle: areas where we are invited to yield. And sometimes the entanglements are things that actually look godly and noble, and they can rob us of our destiny just the same. When we begin to filter out these seemingly godly "obligations," we are creating margin in our lives to live out our identity and our calling. Unfortunately, when we start filtering, we have to say no to people. We have to say no to the sign-up sheet at church. There was a time when we lived off of sign-up sheets, and it was necessary. God was preparing our hearts for everything He would eventually reveal to us about our destiny. But now, now that our destiny is revealed, we say no. We begin to filter out the obligations, and filter in the opportunities. We recognize when ministry opportunities hit our radar that fit our spiritual role, our spiritual gifts, and our passions, and we look to join the Lord where He is at work.

When we live this way, saying, "Yes!" to the Spirit's invitations, and, "No!" to entanglements, we are bound to ruffle feathers. Many people will not understand this way of life. Spiritual authority is a delicate matter. You see, it comes across as super-confident, yet it is completely based in humility. It has to be—it is the only way it works; *He must increase, I must decrease.* The confidence of authority can be misinterpreted as arrogance.

As a friend and I were praying about this very thing some years ago, we asked the Lord how to balance authority with humility. I remember clearly, He gave us Acts 3 as an answer. It is a story about the newly emerged Peter, formerly Simon, who was now beginning to live out his destiny and the authority that came with it. You may recall the story—Peter and John have gone to the temple, where a disabled beggar would daily ask for donations. This day being no different, he asked Peter and John for money. Peter's response is what the Lord highlighted for us. Peter *"fixed his gaze on him and said, 'Look at us!'"* Of course, it was after the man had given them his attention that Peter uttered the famous line, *"I do not have silver and gold, but what I do have I give to you: In the name of Jesus Christ the Nazarene: Walk!"*

It fascinates me that Peter first told the man to look at him. This was a very personal engagement. It required all of the man. It required all of Peter. The man had to focus on Peter.

Now, just to be sure no one thinks we are headed down a path of self-aggrandizement, we have to read the outcome of the story. "With a leap he stood upright and he entered the temple with them, walking and leaping and praising God. And all the people saw him walking and praising God..."

This is the outcome of a child of God who walks in boldness and alignment with the heart of God: we stand in authority, amazing things happen, and God gets all the credit. Period.

The Apostle Paul even has to remind the Corinthians of this in 2 Corinthians 10:7-18, where he says things like, *"For even if I boast somewhat further about our authority, which the Lord gave for building you up and not for destroying you, I will not be put to shame..."* and *"We will not boast beyond our measure, but within the measure of the sphere which God apportioned to us as a measure..."* and finally, *"He who boasts is to boast in the Lord."*

Paul isn't apologizing for coming across as confident or authoritative. He simply reminds people why he is so confident, and where that confidence comes from. He reminds people that it all comes from God and all glory belongs to Him. This, my friends, is how authority in humility, and humility in authority, behaves.

# Conclusion

Why does God give us authority? It would be easy to come up with reasons that have to do with exercising gifts and bearing fruit. But, the Scriptures give a pretty succinct explanation.

God grants authority for a specific *outward* reason—He wants to amaze people to the point that they praise and glorify Him. Time after time, as we read stories of true authority and movement of the Holy Spirit, the inevitable result is an outpouring of adoration to God. As just one of many, many examples, in Matthew 9, Jesus tells the paralytic, "Get up, pick up your bed and go home." The man gets up and goes, and when everyone sees it, the crowd goes wild! *"They were awestruck, and glorified God, who had given such authority to men."* Wow! God is so good to invite us into His process!

God also grants authority for a specific *inward* reason. He thoroughly wants us to experience oneness, togetherness, and immersion, into Himself. One way He does this is by inviting us to participate, on His terms, in His amazing business. Jesus prayed in John 17, *"The glory (esteem) which You have given Me I have given to them, that they may be one, just as We are one...so that the world may know that You sent Me, and loved them, even as You have loved Me. For this is eternal life, that they may know You, the only true God, and Jesus Christ, whom You sent."*

My heart pounds with these words! The Father loves us just like He loves Jesus! Jesus has given us the same esteem that the Father gave Him! They want us to be in Them, and in doing so, we have eternal life. It is almost too much to take in. Thank you, Father, for including us in your unspeakable ways!

# Chapter thirteen

# Calling

Prince Valiant and Princess Sarah lived out their adult years ruling the very domain they had helped to liberate. They worked in tandem, one complementing the other; as he ruled the forest, she ruled the fields.

Dragons did make their assault several times upon the wall over the course of many years. But they could not penetrate the domain of the king under Valiant and Sarah's watch.

Valiant began a great replanting campaign within the forest, to ensure that each generation would have the blessing of trees, and under his care, the forest grew taller and deeper and healthier than before.

Sarah planted rows and rows of vegetables and herbs, and groves of fruit and nut trees. Where there was once only the leftovers of wilted produce and stale bread, she brought forth from the earth nourishing fruit and vegetables for the kingdom's citizens.

Many of the former orphans returned back into the forest and fields, but now, to tend to its health and fruitfulness, and to enjoy the redemption of their home and heritage.

The borders of the kingdom had spread due to the faithfulness of Valiant and Sarah, and it continued to expand on all fronts, as more and more soldiers were crowned *princes and princesses.*

King Avinu was well pleased with Valiant and Sarah. He would spend innumerable hours resting among the shady trees with Valiant. He especially loved gardening with Sarah. Sometimes together, and sometimes alone, the two siblings lived out their days in the good favor of King Avinu, Prince Proto, and Donatella.

## Reading between the lines

This is the happily-ever-after portion of our story. Valiant and Sarah live out their days safeguarding and stewarding the territory that King Avinu gave them responsibility over. Some days called for planting and creating fruitfulness within the kingdom. Other days called for them to care for their brothers and sisters in the faith. And yes, some days called for a fight as they defended the kingdom against attack.

But ultimately, life became much more about *being* than *doing*. Yes, there were responsibilities and duties. Life went on. But it wasn't defined by the labor of their rule, rather it was characterized by a communing and fellowship with the King that simply became the filter that all of life happened through.

Valiant and Sarah were deeply fulfilled in their Kingdom assignments, in large part because the roles were tailored specifically for them. Since they were faithful with the small missions, and because they could be trusted to listen to the direction of the Holy Spirit, and due to the fact that they bore fruit, the King could trust them with their great assignments.

## What is your great kingdom assignment?

Calling is often presented as a mystery. I frequently hear it represented at a conceptual level, with no real clarity as to *how* we engage in it. For this reason, we want to include a discussion of calling in the context of the journey we have been on: the journey out of False Self, and into True Identity. If True Identity is the understanding of who you are, uniquely designed by your Father, and authority is the boldness you develop after beginning to live that identity, then calling is your unique assignment. Life questions begin to fall into place when you know the answers to these questions. True Identity answers the *who* question, "Who am I?" Authority answers the *how* question, "How am I to live out this identity?" And calling answers the *what* question, "What was I put here for?"

## What is Calling?

Calling is another word for *invitation*. God's calling for us is His invitation to us. Now, just like with True Identity, there are different levels of calling. There is calling that is more general and applies to all of God's children, and then there is specific calling that applies directly to an individual. God invites *all* His children generally, and He invites *each* of His children specifically. What does God call, or invite, *all* His children into? Among other things:

### Fellowship with Jesus Christ
*"God is faithful, through whom you were called into fellowship with His Son, Jesus Christ our Lord" 1 Corinthians 1:9.*

**Freedom**
*"For you were called to freedom, brethren; only do not turn your freedom into an opportunity for the flesh, but through love serve one another"* *Galatians 5:13.*

**Holiness**
*"As obedient children, do not be conformed to the former lusts which were yours in your ignorance, but like the Holy One who called you, be holy yourselves also in all your behavior; because it is written, "YOU SHALL BE HOLY, FOR I AM HOLY"* 1 Peter 1:14-16.*

These truths apply to each one of us. These are collectively the general calling that we all share. But what about individual calling? What are you and I uniquely called into?

## How are we called?

Calling is your assignment. This is not hard to imagine; what *is* hard is the discovery. I remember being personally frustrated over this process, and my observation is that our churches are full of people in the same place. How is a person to determine their calling? The Scriptures present a few different ways this can unfold.

**It is assumed**
Many folks in the Church today equate calling with the words that Jesus uttered before His ascension. While they were spoken to His disciples, we have taken them on to apply to us as well. We call His words The Great Commission. *"Go therefore and make disciples of all the nations, baptizing them in the name of the Father and the Son and the Holy Spirit, teaching them to observe all that I commanded you; and lo, I am with you always, even to the end of the age"* Matthew 28:19,20.

**It is automatic**
In Romans 1, Paul the apostle reaffirms to his readers that he is called by God to preach the gospel to the Gentiles. He then goes a step further to include his audience in that same calling. He reminds us that, as saints, we are called, just as he is: *"You also are the called of Jesus Christ."*

**It is able to be deduced**
Luke writes about how Paul had a vision one night. In it, a man was pleading for him to come to Macedonia and help them. Luke then describes the discernment the Apostles used in applying the details of this vision. *"When he had seen the vision, immediately we sought to go into Macedonia, concluding that God had called us to preach the gospel to them"* Acts 16:9.

**It is administered by the Holy Spirit**
Luke also writes about the early church at Antioch which contained certain prophets and teachers, Barnabas being one of them. These people were fasting and ministering to the Lord when the Holy Spirit spoke and said, *"Set apart for Me Barnabas and Saul for the work to which I have called them"* Acts 13:2. They then laid hands on them and prayed for them, and sent them off to where the Holy Spirit was directing them: Cyprus.

Do you notice anything interesting here? What these scriptures describe are varying levels of calling. The first one, or the Great Commission, is the most general form of calling—we are sent to the whole world. The second one is more specific—Paul reminds his readers that they are called to reach the Gentiles. The third level is to a distinct place or group of people, and we see the examples of Macedonia and Cyprus.

Calling is specific to the person being called. Jesus called His disciples to create disciples throughout the world. More specifically, the Holy Spirit called Barnabas and Paul to Cyprus. The Holy Spirit could have called Peter and Philip to Cyprus, or any other combination of apostles. But He didn't. He invited two specific people, and He wanted them specially because He had already gifted them and designed them for this assignment. The same is true for us.

Calling is based in passion, so an obvious question to ask ourselves is, "What am I passionate about?" This is a surprisingly difficult question for many to answer. It requires sifting through our interests, and defining the difference between interests and passions. Passions, in this context, are the deep longings that God has written upon our hearts, perhaps yet to be discovered, longings that are our inspiration toward our destiny.

I remember feeling such guilt over the fact that I did not experience any real passion for evangelism. This guilt is a central theme for many Christians, especially when churches hammer this home as our Christian duty. "If you aren't out evangelizing, you are a bad Christian." Looking back, it should have been clear to me much sooner; my heart came alive when I had opportunities to build up the Body of Christ. And the opportunities kept coming in this area, not in evangelism. Yes, the Lord has used me to evangelize, but the overriding majority of opportunity and fulfillment comes when I am involved in discipleship! What freedom came when I finally understood that I was wired for this! To this day, discipleship is a primary filter through which I assess opportunities to determine if they are *my* opportunities. I love to help the Body grow.

Furthermore, calling has a lifelong design element to it. For me, I am to be writing and speaking, the Lord has made this quite clear to me. Desiree is to be ministering in prayer. You too have a pattern to how God has designed you and how He frequently uses you. What have you observed in this area of your own life?

Finally, this passion that I have for my brothers and sisters, and the knowledge that I am to write and to speak, are further filtered by the season that the Lord has called me to. Over a seven-year period, between 2009 and 2015, I counted six different seasons, or times of specific calling to specific people for a specific time period. This seasonality is meant to allow us to ebb and flow, to move and respond with the Lord as He works in different places and times and for varied purposes. Have you noticed a shift from season to season, in who God was drawing you to, and in why He was drawing you to them? Have you experienced the need to prepare differently for changing seasons of calling?

## Why are we called?

It is easy to speculate about why we are called. We could say that we are called because we are God's hands and feet here on earth. Ok, sure, that is true, but is that really the core of why we are called?

If a major theme of the New Testament is that Jesus came to make a way for us to know our Father—the very same Father who predesigned and predestined us, the same Father who called us His own because of His kind affection toward us, then perhaps our calling is also part of this tender connection with our Father. What does Scripture have to say about this?

**We are called so we may inherit blessing:** 1 Peter 3:8,9
*"...you were called for the very purpose that you might inherit a blessing"*

**We are called so that God's pleasure may be revealed in us:** Galatians 1:15-17
*"But when God, who had...called me through His grace, was pleased to reveal His Son in me so that I might preach Him among the Gentiles..."*

**We are called so that we may gain the glory of Jesus:** 2 Thess 2:13-17
*"...He called you through our gospel, that you may gain the glory of our Lord Jesus Christ..."*

**We are honored by God:** Hebrews 5:1-5
*"...no one takes the honor to himself, but receives it when he is called by God..."*

**We are created with deep purpose:** 2 Timothy 1:8-12
*"...God, who has saved us and called us with a holy calling, not according to our works, but according to His own purpose..."*

## What is expected of those who are called?

The old corporate adage is that people have three inherent questions when it comes to what is expected of them. "What am I supposed to be doing? How am I supposed to be doing it? How am I doing at it?" And lastly, "What can I expect for doing so?" Some of this same questioning applies to our calling. What is expected of us? There are a couple of indications from the Scriptures.

**We are to carry ourselves in a respectful manner:** Ephesians 4:1-3
*"...walk in a manner worthy of the calling with which you have been called..."*

**We are to produce fruit where God has us:** 1 Corinthians 7:17-22
*"Each man must remain in that condition in which he was called. Were you called while a slave? Do not worry about it; but if you are able also to become free, rather do that..."*

## Why are we afraid of Calling?

An unfortunate, yet consistent perspective that Christians have is that we are afraid of our calling. We are afraid that God will tell us to go somewhere we don't want to go and to do something we don't want to do. We are afraid that God will want us to help people we don't like. We are afraid that God will make us get rid of all of our stuff. We have many fears.

We don't want to be the proverbial square peg that is hammered and forced into a place where it doesn't fit. And so, millions upon millions of believers avoid this conversation with God. And, unsurprisingly, we are far too often miserable as we miss out on the very reason for our existence.

These fears reveal our lack of understanding our Father. On one hand, we don't understand Him because we do not know Him intimately. On the other hand, we don't understand Him because our spiritual heritage has not prepared us for connection with Him.

When we get to know the Father, His heart becomes familiar. And as a result, in the words of 1 John 4:18, His perfect love resolves our fears: including our fear of what He may ask us to do.

The reality of His love is that He wired us for the very thing He has purposed us to do! In other words, we do what we love! What do we love? We love and hurt for the people that He grants us a love for. We love and long for the place that He beckons us to.

Calling is frustrating to discover because we are not ready to do what we love as long as we love our agendas more than His. He has to continually invite us further into Himself where there is no need for (or room for) our agendas. This process can take a while, and often moves in relation to our willingness to yield to Him.

As we consider the "spiritual giants" we immortalize, their stories tend to follow similar paths. They commonly have to face a crisis of faith, or a major trial, or a costly act of yielding that serves to minimize their own agendas and bring to the forefront God's plans and purposes. And, for the rest of their lives it seems they are 100% sold out to a singular cause for the kingdom of God.

This, my friends, is what calling looks like. Once discovered, you cannot go back. What would you go back to? How could you ever stop? You were made for it!

## Conclusion

King Solomon could well be a spokesman for much of the journey we have embarked upon. He, in his own words, indulged in every pleasure accessible to him, learned everything he could learn, and achieved far more than most of us ever could. And upon reflection, he determined that it was all empty and fruitless.

He goes on to propose a truth that I believe summarizes what we have been talking about here. He writes that God has put eternity in our hearts: that He has embossed, at our core, a secret inclusion into His good and eternal work. Regarding God's people, he states, *"I know that there is nothing better for them than to rejoice and to do good in one's lifetime,"* and there is *"good in all his labor—it is the gift of God."* And to Solomon's reassurance and desire to leave a lasting legacy, he proclaims of our participation in God's work, *"I know that everything God does will remain forever..."*

There is a great fulfillment and confident peace that exists when we know that we are living out the identity, role, and assignment that our Father has for us. That is not to say that it will always be pleasant or easy, but there is nothing that compares with the sense of acceptance that comes with it.

I would encourage you to explore the hangups and the fears, the facades and the barriers, that keep you from experiencing intimacy with your heavenly Father. I challenge you to believe that He sees you as His masterpiece, created for His good purposes. And finally, I pray that you will experience the richness of His thoughts toward you, and the abundant life that results from embracing your True Identity.

Who are you, and why are you here?

---

* Ecc 3:11-14

# Mastering Time for Productivity

## A Guide to Improve Efficiency in Work and Life

Harness Task Management,
Conquer Procrastination and
Achieve Balance

**ELLEN SEDGE**

Impisi™ Media LLC
Smart Work-Life Series